Fishing the Dust of Kenya

G.E. Johnson

1

Fishing the Dust of Kenya

© 2022 G.E. Johnson

Distributed by Adriel Publishing

Printed in the U.S.A.

Cover design by Hatice Bayramoglu and Liz Lawless

ISBN: 979-8-9872132-0-9

*To the God who leads me
and the people of Kenya whose smiles
and friendship will stay with me
for the rest of my days.*

Fishing The Dust of Kenya

Note to the Readers:
Many names and places mentioned here are spelled phonetically only. In many cases we were introduced to people only on a first name basis. When a last name was given or a place identified, it was not pronounced clearly or spelled out for us. Even if it had been, we did not have our journals with us in the field.

Key Persons in each Chapter

Shem Okla = Volunteer Coordinator Baptist Ministries & Preacher = Chapter 1, 6, 10

Bob Calvert = Baptist Missionary working among Maasai = Chapter 2

Samuel Tiana = very tall Elder of Maasai Boma working with Bob Calvert = Chapter 2

Peter and Eunice = Maasai Translators = Chapter 2

Jackson = small man First Preacher Missioner's heard = Chapter 2

Maasai Warrior Scholar = Studied Wildlife Conservation in California, Maasai Scholar Lecturer & Lead Dancer and Horn Player = Chapter 2, 5, & 6

Miss Lucy and Husband David = Pehucci Orphanage = Chapter 3

Mary = Cook at Pehucci Orphanage, Chapter 3

Dr. Cathryn = Maasia Doctor who went with Missioner's to Pehucci = Chapter 3 & 10

Bishop James Mbai = Poppa Leader of the Tent Mission = Chapter 4, 12, & 13

Gideon = Poppa's Right Hand Man at Tent Mission = Chapter 4 & 10

Joy Kirschner = USA Missioner Leader = Chapter 4 & 8

Washington = Male Teacher Tent Mission = Chapter 4

Joyce = Cook at Tent Mission = Chapter 4

Dancing Robinson = Another Preacher at Tent Mission = Chapter 4

John = Maasai Safari Driver = Chapter 5

Ruth Okla = Shem's wife and high school teacher = Chapter 5

Mike = Cattleman & Member of Missioner Team = Chapter 6

Uncle Byron = Author's Favorite Uncle Who Trained Air Force Pilots = Chapter 7

Frances Farmer = Life Partner = Chapter 8

God-loving People = Chapter 9

Father Neel = Author's Priest at Holy Trinity By The Lake and Who started this Missioner Trip = Chapter 9

Friends = Chapter 10

Prayer Warriors = Chapter 10

Paul Simon & Art Garfunkel = Musicians = Chapter 11

Led Zepplin = Musicians = Chapter 11

Steppenwolf = Musicians = Chapter 11

Brian Becker = Church Friend of Author = Chapter 12

Cardiologist = Performed Surgery on Bishop Mbai = Chapter 12

Florence Mbai = Bishop's Wife = Chapter 13

Lameck Mbai = Bishop's Son = Chapter 13

Elijah = 5-year-old Tent Boy = Chapter 13

Table of Contents

Prequel—The Reluctant Missioner

How did I end up in Nairobi? I often ask myself that question, and it is not an easy one to answer. The "trip" toward the decision to go was a much harder trip than the 21 hour flight. And it all started with a mysterious email from someone I had never heard of or met. She somehow knew my name, though, and put me on an email list to inquire whether or not I would be interested in going on a mission trip to Kenya with an organization called Living Water International (LWI). I laughed; in fact, I laughed out loud at the thought of myself as a missioner. But I thought, too, why not? It could be a once-in-a-lifetime trip. So I did my research on LWI and found a truly remarkable mission...providing clean water in third world communities along with supplying the gospel of the Living Water, Christ himself.

The email quoted Christ: *"Who will go for me? Whom shall I send?"* Somehow it struck a chord, but I immediately dismissed the idea of going that far from home with people I didn't even know, to go see and live among people I didn't know. I am no good at holding conversations with strangers, and the LWI mission teams are made up of people from all across the United States. They go into highly impoverished and undeveloped areas not only to provide access to clean water, but to talk evangelism as well. I didn't even talk to my own family about my religious beliefs and feelings; why would I talk to strangers about those things? Religion was a private thing to me...something between just God and me. I was comfortable with things that way. But I was soon to be shoved out of my comfort zone.

The decision to go involved much wrangling with myself. I expected my family to throw a fit. They didn't. I expected to ignore the invitation to go. I couldn't. I expected my relationship with God to stay the same. It wouldn't. I ran through indecisiveness, frustration, disappointment, anger (because I was being compelled to go when I did not want to go and God was not accepting no as an answer.) I cried. A lot! I wiggled and waffled and wavered; and every time I thought, *"No, I am not going,"* a song would enter my head and loop over and over, a blasted earworm! It was the hymn with words, *"Where streams of living waters flow, my ransomed soul He leadeth.*" And it would play in my head over and over and over and over.

I went through at least fifty reasons not to go. There were too many things that could go wrong. After all, Africa is known for its snakes and its poison dart tree frogs, and let's not forget the lions! Kenya, I just knew, would have icky food that I would not like. There would be filth and disease and pure, raw poverty everywhere with nothing to soften it. Getting there and being there were both dangerous enterprises. Terrorists commandeering the overseas flight could not be discounted. The thought of going on this trip opened up my entire little toy chest of horrors. I was afraid. Plus I have grown into a creature of comfort who has worked hard over the years to overcome unsafe and unsavory living conditions. I had done the hard road of life. I did not want to travel that road again. But more than anything else, I was afraid that a lion or a terrorist would kill me. As silly as that all sounds, at the time it was a very real fear...fear that gripped me to the core, fear that I was headed toward my doom.

So I began arguing with God about the whole situation, like you can win an argument with God! Ha! I questioned Him: "*Are You sure you have the right Johnson? Are You crazy trying to make a missioner out of me? Who am I to be sent on so important a job? Don't You know I am not equipped for this kind of work?*

Besides, I cuss! You've heard me! I drink and dance, and there will be Baptists in the group. That won't work. Don't You realize, God, that making a missioner out of me is the proverbial equivalent of making a silk purse out of a sow's ear? What a strange sense of humor You have!"

For every argument though, there was the earworm song reminding me..."*where streams of living waters flow.*" So as I entered into this true spiritual struggle, as I threw up barricades, God removed every single barrier, straightened every kink, moved aside every boulder. He dogged me like that horse and rider do the small steer when calf roping in a rodeo. At the end of two weeks, I was exhausted. But He had worked up a sweat, too! I had no idea why God was calling me to Kenya, and while I could think of 50 reasons not to go, there were four really good reasons TO go.

The first was the fulcrum of Christ himself to balance me. Then there was the Fountain of Life that is Christ to wash away the fears and anxieties. There was also the prospect of fishing, and I love fishing. I was just going to fish for a different kind of *"fish"*. As the saying goes, *"You catch 'em. God will clean 'em."* Besides, Moses didn't win his argument about going to Egypt to free the Israelites. If Moses couldn't win his arguments, there was no way I was going to. So it all boiled down to simple faith...did I trust God in this plan? And that is when I decided to *"cowboy up"* – and go.

On this trip we were to take designated things needed for the mission: school and clinic supplies, books, clothing, hygiene supplies, toys, puppets, musical instruments, and an array of other things. We could take two large trunks filled with these things, and one carry-on bag. We were to leave everything behind when we left except for our carry-on and the one set of clothes we would wear to come home. I fell in love with that idea, and went to work on collecting the things I wanted to take and give away.

By the time October rolled around, I was still a basket case of fear, but I was going in spite of it. The trunks were loaded. I had 19 sets of children's clothes, 20 flute recorders, 8 sets of scrubs, 90 toothbrushes, 55 pounds of books, 30 bars of soap, 120 pens and 70 pencils, numerous medical supplies, a CD player, CD's of children's Bible songs, and batteries to power our way to sing along for the Lord.

Benefactors had stepped forward. I had spent $700 on shots for typhoid, diphtheria, polio, yellow fever, tetanus, measles-mumps-rubella, and hepatitis A and B. I had spent $145 for an expedited passport. The $2,700 for air fare, room, and board had been donated. I had a friend ready to take me to the airport. Kenya was waiting. I was ready to fish.

Departure Thoughts

Dear Family and Friends,

I stand at my garage door and stare at the luggage about to go out. A friend will arrive early in the morning to drive me to DFW International Airport for my first trip overseas. My heart does one big belly-flop as my brain silently rolls the word *"international"* through the synapses. I am on the verge of the largest precipice of my life, about to leap into the Total Unknown, in a country as foreign to me as papyrus, pagodas, and penguins, Soho, Swahili, and saccharine. (You know I always say, *"You can't ever have too much sugar."*)

While I have some knowledge of these things, I don't KNOW these things. But God has a plan that includes my active dedication to duty and a commitment to His call. Since He knows me as a life-long learner, He has chosen to bless me by teaching me innumerable things even beyond my own vigorous and energetic imagination, and the thrills and passions of my heart. I anticipate learning what it means to...

I leave that statement open to all possibilities and simply trust the promise, *"I will instruct you and teach you in the way you should go; I will counsel you and watch over you."* (Psalms 32:8) Tennyson also reminds me, *"Closer is He than breathing, and nearer than hands and feet."*

I know many of you are concerned about my safety and that of the team; and believe me, my extremely ebullient imagination has led me through some very dark, tearful, and fearful hours leading up to this departure. But as I step out the door tomorrow morning, my heart is brave and calm. More than praying for a successful mission, more than praying for my usefulness to others, more than praying for no snakes...

I have prayed for courage. Knowing that it is fear, more than anything else, that holds us back from our dreams, our goals, the living out of our lives with great energy and purpose and yes, even true risks, I have chosen to ignore my consternation and disquietude and to answer the call given to me. Your support, dear family and friends, has made that an easy, though somewhat uncomfortable, decision. So more than anything else, I have prayed for courage, and at various times in various ways, I have seen it in many of you. That is how I was able to recognize it when the courage I had lost came back home to me.

I know how hard it is for some of you to see me go, but I firmly believe we are born to live extraordinary lives in testament to the incomparable God who made us. I also firmly believe my life to this point HAS indeed been extraordinary, but there is more life to live. So please know that I am going with great certainty and purpose and with a happy, giving heart. I am always happiest when I have a chance to give something. So even though I understand your concerns, and have shared some of them myself, I leave you with the same assurance as that which is given to me at this time: *"Along unfamiliar paths I will guide them; I will turn darkness into light before them and make the rough places smooth."* (Isaiah 42:16)

So, Dear Ones, as I step out of my garage, as I step out onto the breezeway to the airplane, as I wing across the ocean mighty and deep, as I set foot on foreign soil among strangers in need, I am confident my blessings, as many as they are already, will increase in numbers beyond accounting. Only now, at this moment of writing, do I understand for the first time the math concept of imaginary numbers. I am confident, too, that you will be blessed beyond measure for sharing this journey with me.

"My prayer for you is that you overflow more and more with love for others, and at the same time keep on

growing in spiritual knowledge and insight." (Philippians 1:9)

AND –– *"Above all, love one another deeply, because love covers over a multitude of sins."* (1 Peter 4:8) Cowboy Up! With love and prayers, gej

Chapter 1
Welcome to Nairobi

As I sit to begin my writing, to put my footsteps into words, to condense over 21,000 miles into a few pages, to give you a look at a land so unlike anything we know here, the task seems highly daunting, almost Herculean in scope. However, when I think of the tasks the Kenyans take on each day, my writing difficulties seem trivial. As strong and powerful as my writing can be at times, it in no way will ever landscape the city or characterize the people as they really are. Even when you see it with your very own eyes, you cannot believe what you see. You expect to see abject poverty and a people beaten to the ground by it and with no hope. What you find are people of great love and great spirit, who pray with such earnest hearts for the needs of others but rarely for themselves, except in great thanksgiving for what they do actually have, little as it is. They realize that what they do have is more than what someone else has, and each and every day is a good day made by the Lord and given to them, and they are grateful beyond measure. They are a hopeful people, a gentle people with soft-spoken, unhurried voices, who look daily for some way to serve the Lord by helping a neighbor.

Kenya is a country that has no sense of modern time, however, and that is not necessarily a bad thing. Just like in Las Vegas, clocks are a rarity. Things like meetings and appointments run on what the people there call *"African time"*, meaning it is not unusual to wait 3 hours for the arrival of an expected friend or guest. Time is of no essence there; it is not the ruler of life that it is here in America. Oddly enough though, while hours and minutes have little impact on daily living, in Nairobi traffic, life is lived by mere inches and half inches as a vehicle weaves it way through hundreds of pedestrians, bicycles, carts pushed or pulled by people or animals, goats herded along the medians of main highways and thoroughfares, the air filled to capacity with dust, smoke from burning garbage heaps, and exhaust from poorly maintained automobiles and trucks. Nairobi is a bustling, active, energetic city where space of any kind is a premium, so an inch here and a half inch there is handled with a skill of movement unmatched by any *"controlled chaos"* seen on the streets and freeways of America. As a friend I met in Nairobi told me, *"Driving in Nairobi will change your prayer life."* He says this with a big smile and an embracing laugh. His name is Shem Okala. He is one of a dozen or more people I will introduce to you as you read through this travel account. Each one of these friends inspired me beyond measure and humbled me in the way each one approached life in Kenya, the needs of the people there, and their personal contributions, visions, and sacrifices that are a daily part of how they are building the body of Christ.

Nairobi is a city of 3 and half million people, 75% of them unemployed. Even during our nation's greatest financial crisis, the Great Depression of the 1930's, our largest percent of unemployment was only 25%. So that gives you a point of reference for comparison regarding the dire situation in Kenya. Each day in Africa 5,500 children die from diseases borne from unclean drinking water. HIV/Aids kills thousands more. Thousands of children are orphaned or living on the streets, some of them as young as 6 or 7 years old. Their parents have died from aids or some other dysentery-type disease, or the parents have turned them out into the streets to survive on their own because the parents cannot feed and care for them. The vast majority of the children though usually become common thieves to survive, hoping that whatever food they steal will not be taken from them by older children or adults. The street life is a very hard life for anyone, as you might imagine; but for a child 6-10 years old, it is one living nightmare after another. Prayers are answered when an orphanage or a street mission takes in the child. The general perception is that the Maasai people living out in the remote areas are living the hard life, but ones we met seem much happier and healthier than the many people in Nairobi. The Maasai have the pastoral life, which has its own hardships, but the stress level of day-today survival does not seem as evident.

In every area of the city and the surrounding neighborhoods, everyone lives like virtual prisoners. Every house or orphanage or school or mission compound or guest house is surrounded by a 6 foot fence. If you are well off, your 6 foot fence is constructed of cinder blocks or brick. If poor, the fence is either pieces of sheet metal nailed or tied together or made of wooden poles and sticks. Every fence has a double iron gate of some type, some quite elaborate. The gate has a sliding rectangular peep hole so the watchman can see who is at the gate before opening it. The gate also has a doorway cut in it so a person can walk out of the gate without opening it. Then, of course, the gate can be fully opened to allow a vehicle to enter the property. Inside the house, sections are partitioned off by wrought iron locking doors or full metal doors. This setup seems designed to restrict access to all areas of the house should any would be robbers gain entry. These cordoned areas would prevent the robbers from ransacking the entire house.

Neighborhoods have gatekeepers at barricades to the entry of the area. Many people have watchmen at their gates. If the watchman does his job well, safety is maintained and the stress decreases proportionally.

Despite all the slums and city problems, such as no water infrastructure, Nairobi does have its beauty marks. There are areas where coffee bean plantations are farmed in the middle of neighborhoods, palm trees line the streets, vibrant colors of clothing and foliage intermingle with the dusty red dirt footpaths. The purple flowering jacaranda trees provide an exotic beauty to the city that makes it seem almost an illusion. The trees and bushes flower in bright reds, orange, brilliant yellows, pinks, and purples. Part of the beauty is created, too, by numerous roadside nurseries that sell any type of plant imaginable. These roadside nurseries are everywhere and seemingly do a good business since there is so little overhead expense. There is no building necessary to house the plants. All that is needed is enough workers to watch to ensure no theft of the plants.

The total effect is that the mind almost feels like it is incapacitated by some hallucinogen because the contrasts are so stark. Trying to reconcile the brown and tan dirt and the black plastic and burning rubber colors of poverty with the gracious elegance of the greenery and calypso colors is much like mixing oil and water. It just does not make much sense to the senses that in one second of sight you see canary yellow flowers on the tree by the street and underneath the tree is a smoldering, smoking garbage pile being picked over by a small group of emaciated women and a toddler or two alongside. You learn that most children die within the first two years of birth, and for that reason, the people usually do not even name their children until they reach at least two years of age. So everything you see, hear, smell, feel, and taste has a contradiction to it. Nairobi is the living, breathing city that survives on the rule of physics that for every action there is an equal and opposite reaction. The prime example of this concept is seen in the contrast of the living conditions with the spiritual living. Despite horrendous conditions, the people by nature think little about themselves and typically pray about the needs of others. Despite a general fear of strangers who might be potential robbers, the people would approach us and would not ask for money. Instead they would ask that we take their greetings and blessings back to our families who were kind enough to share us with them in their country.

Colors of Nairobi

Security Gate at Karina's Guest House

Chapter 2
The Maasai People, Past, and Present

Since we arrived late Saturday night, our first real visual look at the city came our first Sunday morning in Kenya as we headed out of the city into MaasaiLand. It was a strange site seeing all those people bustling around on foot, dressed in their best clothes, scurrying off to worship, kicking up red dust all along the way with the help of the goats grazing in the medians. Then suddenly we were passing the site of the old U.S. Embassy that was bombed in 1998, killing about 200 people. I know I suddenly felt the realism of the danger since the new embassy had just reopened a few days before our arrival. It had been closed almost four months, since late June, because of specific threats linked to al Qaeda terrorists. It was a sobering moment with a quick prayer.

We made a rendezvous to meet a Baptist missionary named Bob Calvert who has been working among the

Maasai for the past several years and who has been highly successful in assimilating himself and his family into the culture of MaasaiLand. Several churches have been established, and we worshipped at one of the Maasai churches this first Sunday in Kenya. The church itself was only 2-3 years old, but already it had established itself as a mother church and had started other mission churches within approximately a 50-mile radius. Fifty miles does not seem like much area, but when you consider that these people walk everywhere, things come into perspective. Many of the people who worshipped with us that morning had walked 4-5 miles to attend church, after they had gotten up to do chores and water their animals. How many Americans would walk that walk if that is what they had to do to get to church on Sunday? I have to be honest and say I am too much a creature of comfort, and it makes me tired even to think about walking 4-5 miles to go anywhere!

It was interesting to note that the little church we attended is a Baptist established church, but it was quite charismatic in worship. The people trickled in slowly throughout the service because of the long walk and the time it took to care for the herds. But each one arrived with a heart full of praise and much energy for singing. The only instrument in the church was a 3-legged conga drum that kept falling over because one of the legs was bent and kept slipping out of place. This annoyance, however, did not deter the leader or the congregation in the fervent singing of the songs, which were sung in Swahili.

The rhythms and melodies were uplifting, and the people taught us the traditional Maasai dance movements that often accompany the singing. It is a movement of thrusting out the neck and swaying forward and back while slightly bending the knees and stepping forward. Usually a good deal of jumping is part of this worship as well, but they did not jump much at all this particular Sunday. We think perhaps they sensed our reservations; plus as a group, we were still relatively new to each other and unsure what to expect of ourselves as a team. Can you imagine, however, 4 Episcopalians and 2 Baptists clapping their hands, sway dancing, and jumping up and down while singing *"On Christ the Solid Rock I Stand"?* It just was not going to happen! We loosened up as best we could, but we obviously were not ready for praise and worship that is so overtly demonstrative and physical. The other 2 in our group of 8 are from community churches that are Baptist-based but are a bit more charismatic than the usual Baptists, so they got into the worship more freely than we other 6 did.

It was a rather funny predicament also because we did not know what songs they were singing. Some of the songs were translated for us, but only a few of the 20 or so that were sung. Yes, the Maasai are a singing bunch!

So I found myself making up my own translations for the Swahili songs I was hearing. I thank God so much that I have that kind of creative mind that I can do things like that at times when I lack understanding. It kept me involved with what was going on around me and helped me construct some meaning connected to the worship. The Maasai voices around us were absolutely lyrical and joyous beyond belief, and everyone knew all the songs from memory. The singing was strong and loud, and the preaching was energetic and fervent. I am sure the Lord smiled upon their worship that morning (and even snickered a little at us 8 trying to keep up with these energetic tribal people.)

Aside from our mission leader, none of us had ever had any contact with the Maasai, and their experience with white people had been equally limited. Bob Calvert was not with us because he and the elder of the boma, a very tall thin man named Samuel Tiana, were going *"over the hill"* several miles away to worship at one of the newly formed mission churches started by this mother church. Bob introduced us to a young Maasai man named Peter who would be one of our translators. Peter had just graduated *"from university"* as they phrase it, and he spoke very good English. He was able to go to college because he had worked as a driller for several years for Living Water International (LWI), and the organization helped him with finances. Peter led most of the singing and explained the dancing and nature of worship. The sermon was preached by a small man named Jackson and translated for us by a young woman named Eunice who attends college somewhere in Kenya. That is something quite unusual for a Maasai girl, but she was a true delight to us and to her people.

After church we rode out to Peter's boma and met his entire family. The boma, of course, like all Maasai villages, was surrounded by a thorn thicket fence to protect the people and herd, which is kept at night in the center of the village. The main predator is the lion. We were invited into one home so we could see what it is like inside. The house is constructed of sticks, mud, and cow dung, and it stands no taller than maybe 5 ft. Inside is completely dark except for the little bit of light coming from the last embers of a fire in the center of the main room. The fire is for cooking and warmth, but it was particularly warm that day. Entering the house was like walking a maze because there is a zigzag entryway. The houses are built this way so that if a lion should enter the boma and get into the house, the crooked entry to the main room would confuse the lion and hopefully he will back out of the door rather than proceed through the turns. Peter's house is very different from the others because his education has given him more wealth compared to the others. His house is constructed of wood beam frame covered over with sheet metal and a metal door. It has 3 rooms: one is his study with his desk and books and supplies, the middle room is a living room with a small table and a couple of wooden chairs, and at the other end is the bedroom. He has built the house himself and is hoping to pay a *"bride prize"* soon so he can marry.

On safari we met a young Maasai warrior who has been to the US to college in California to study wildlife conservation. He is currently in disagreement with his family about his first marriage because he is in love with another lady and wants to marry her instead of the bride chosen for him by his family. When he questions them about why it has to be done that way, their answer is, *"You WILL because you MUST."* Tradition dictates every aspect of life among the Maasai, so one MUST because that is how it has always been done and the people have survived doing things that way for generations. The Maasai were interested to know how an American takes a bride and if he must pay a bride prize. When we told them he did not pay, they were astounded! We all had a great laugh though when we told them, *"Oh, he pays alright, just in a different way--like a big diamond ring and an endless list of other equal expectations."*

The most notable thing about the Maasai though is their form of dress and accessorizing. Red is the predominant color of the Maasai attire, and when riding through the countryside of rolling plains where you can see across several miles, it is very easy to spot a Maasai herdsman by the speck of red you will see from quite a distance. Maasai men and women stretch out large holes in their earlobes and decorate their ears with multi-colored beadwork jewelry. They are extremely colorful people in attire and decoration, but the clothing is always dominated by red. When they saw us, one of the Maasai women noted that Americans don't know how to dress up and look pretty! We all looked so plain in our grays and tans, with our hair untidy, little if any makeup, and no jewelry of any kind. Compared to them and the beautifully colored clothing and jewelry they wore, we looked like scraggly chickens in a pen full of peacocks. And compared to their tall, thin frames, we looked like plump dumplings to go with those chickens! One odd thing about the attire stands out though, and that is the wrap that is worn that looks like Scottish clan plaid patterns that are blue and red, sometimes red and white. This wrap is called a shuka, and the patterns were actually introduced to the Maasai by the Scots years ago. The Maasai easily adopted these patterns because of the warmth of the materials and the colorfulness of them. How ironic to have two cultures so different actually share such identifiable clothing associated with both groups.

We also noticed that many of the older men and women were missing some front teeth on the lower jaw.

The Maasai warrior who has been studying in the states explained that the teeth were taken out when very young because lockjaw was so prevalent. Taking the teeth out provided a way to put fluid and food in the mouth to keep them alive. This modern day Maasai had all of his teeth and did not have the large holes in his ears. He had just enough of the Maasai that he was able to function still within his community; but at the same time, he was different enough to function abroad also, combining the best knowledge from both worlds. He spoke out vehemently against female circumcision that is still practiced among the Maasai, but that is a practice not likely to be eliminated from the culture for some time to come even though more and more of the younger generation Maasai are voicing strong opposition.

We also had the opportunity to visit a Maasai school on another day. Things had gotten crossed up in communication, and they were not expecting us at the Enkasiti Primary School as we had anticipated they would be. When we arrived, we all had to sit in the principal's office for an hour-long visit while we had conversation and exchange of questions. This is pretty standard practice in all of Kenya, not just in Maasai-Land. Every meeting begins at the top where you sit and converse and discuss and ruminate before going to the next highest stationed person and repeating the same conversation and discussion and ruminations as you just had with the first. It is not unusual to be at a place for a couple of hours, discussing, before you ever get around to doing the actual business for which you came. But even though we were unexpected, we were welcomed into the school and were given the opportunity to teach some hygiene classes to both the Maasai children and their parents who, by luck, happened to be at the school that day for a kind of PTA meeting! It was very interesting to me, as an educator, that the Maasai were doing things very similarly to things we do here in the USA. They had a mission statement posted on the wall; they had a duty roster posted for the teachers; they were getting parents involved in the school; they were preparing the children for government tests, a la TAKS; the students were even required to wear uniforms. Prior to July, the only students who attended school were children with wealthy parents because parents had to pay for the schooling. The new President of Kenya, who was in the United States meeting with President George W. Bush while we were in Kenya, declared in July that there would be free and compulsory education for all children through grade 8. Many parents were so happy for their children to be attending school for the first time, and the children actually WANT an education, even in MaasaiLand. It just goes to show that education is the only true and lasting solution to ending extreme poverty anywhere.

Meeting the Maasai people was truly a captivating educational experience for me as well as a spiritual one. They are primitive by many of our standards, yet they welcome strangers like long, lost friends. Everyone smiled at us and wanted to shake hands with us. They welcomed us to dance and jump with them. They were proud to show us their homes and cattle. They were infinitely grateful for the water well LWI had placed near their churches and schools. Many still had to herd their animals 4-7 miles to the well, but they used to have to herd them 25-30 miles. They clearly recognized the importance of clean water for both themselves and their animals. With the wells in operation, they have not had to bleed their animals in order to have something to drink during the dry spells. Everyone is healthier, and life in the MaasaiLand is easier and happier. Right now, though, there are over 120 wells approved for drilling but waiting for funding. The wells are very expensive because they have to be dug so deep to get good water. The well site we visited that first Sunday was over 1,000 ft. deep and had cost $30,000 to build. The water tower and the generator to pump the water have to be guarded around the clock because of their value to thieves. It is a great honor to be selected as a well site guard, and the responsibility is tremendous. That one well provides water for over 6,000 people and who knows how many herding animals. The really wonderful thing about the well though is that once constructed, the requirement is that it is deeded to everyone and no one, so all can have access to it. As you may know, people can go without food for quite a long time, but they cannot live more than a few days without water. With the wells being placed at a strategic spots, clean water is available to all around the area. Thanks be to God!

Maasai Matriarch

Congregants at the Maasai Church

Maasai herdsman at a Living Water well site 14

Chapter 3
Pehucci Orphanage

African time took over the day of our first visit to Pehucci (puh-who-chee) because we were scheduled to arrive at 10 am but did not actually get there until 1 pm! There was a mix up with our translators and with the arrangement for the cell phone we were supposed to have. Our translators were told to go to one place different from where we went to pick them up. So we went to the other place where they went, but they were gone by the time we got there. The car they were supposed to use to follow us out to Pechucci had broken down and was in shop. We could not wait any longer, so we went on our own without the translators. Being without translators was only a problem when talking with the very young children because they have not yet learned much English. The older children, however, had a pretty good command of the language. In our two visits with these children, we left with such a strong sense of hope for Kenya.

The orphanage is run by Miss Lucy and her husband David. Miss Lucy is a true human dynamo, a woman with enormous strength of faith and courage. Her orphanage is home to 98 boys and girls, but it is also a resource to the entire little village that surrounds the place. As many as 600 children receive some type of assistance at Pehucci, whether it is schooling, learning a trade, or simply getting water from the LWI water well at the orphanage. The first thing you notice about the children though is that they are so much smaller than their American counterparts. I spent the better part of my time with the middle school aged students who were 13 and 14 but who looked to be 8-9 years old. Despite their stunted growth though, they are every bit as energetic and inquisitive as any other children of comparable age.

The school employs 8 teachers and 1 cook named Mary. In addition to nurturing the 98 children, Miss Lucy is responsible for Mary's being alive today. Mary had been beaten severely by her husband and left for dead with two broken legs. Miss Lucy literally carried Mary on her back to a hospital to get some care for her. When Mary was well enough to leave the hospital, Miss Lucy took Mary home with her and nursed her until she was completely healed, and then she gave her a place to stay at the orphanage by hiring her as the cook. That kind of

Good Samaritan example and leadership is what drives the orphanage and school to the level of success it has. In terms of the other orphanage we visited at the tent mission in Nairobi, the children of Pehucci are miles ahead of them because Miss Lucy has networked with so many in any effort to garner more and more support for the children.

We toured the cookhouse, helped set up and serve the children's lunch, and I visited with some boys who were working out back, making cinder blocks so they can build an open air pavilion to have a place to eat. Vocational education is alive and well! The children had a lunch of rice mush with cornflakes on top. They ate in the yard and ate with their dusty, little fingers. When we returned two days later, one of our team brought them 100 new bowls and 100 spoons so they would not have to eat with their fingers again. We tried to make Miss Lucy promise to throw away the old bowls that are cracked and broken, but she said she would not throw them away because "somewhere there is one who needs a bowl too and does not have even a broken one." After the lunch, we were ushered to a bench in the shade in the courtyard near the flagpole.

This first visit was designed more as a ceremonial visit. We were there to meet the children for the first time, to see how the orphanage and school operates, and to do some Public Relations work. We brought a brand new nylon Christian flag for Pehucci since theirs was tattered and had disintegrated to rags. We could not, however, just take down the old one and run up the new one. *"Noooo, no, no, no!"* as the Kenyans say. They say yes or no answers at least 3 times following the first long answer. But we had to have a big production with a choir performance, a boys dance group performance, and a military-type scout drill to lower the old and raise the new, all while about 400 children stood around the flag pole in the blazing afternoon heat. But just as everything else goes with African time, there was no hurrying through these activities. If I didn't know better, I would swear Miss Lucy and all other Kenyans are closet Episcopalians the way they love pomp and circumstance for any ceremony. :-)

When all the official activities were completed, we then had a prayer, a long prayer, an unhurried prayer, just like the ceremonies. There was one exception though. Prayer was not done standing in the courtyard. It was done in the courtyard, on their knees, in the dirt, each prayer said aloud with a great murmur like the humming of bees, and they were praying for us. They prayed in thanksgiving for our friendship and for our courage in coming so far from home, for our safe journey back home, for many blessings to be given to us. They prayed that we would know the love they have for us, that we would know they will carry us in their hearts and would remember us daily in their prayers. There was never a mention one about their own needs, again just the needs of others, and I don't know when I have ever been more moved by a prayer service in my life.

We had so many things to give to Pehucci that we could not bring it all on the first trip. The van could hold only the 8 of us and the driver, Julius, and we could get only 3 footlockers in the back. Our second trip to Pehucci was to be the truly interactive day with the children. That was the day we brought the other 3 footlockers and did crafts with them, read Bible stories to them in English, did some counseling with them, and just generally hung out with them. The kids and Miss Lucy were just fascinated by the musical instruments we took, especially the lap harp, kazoos, and recorders (a type of flute). We also took some CD's with Sunday school type songs on them and a CD player that runs on batteries. They knew almost all of the Sunday school songs and loved the CD of the Veggie Tales characters singing the songs. Teachers in the country and in the culture are highly respected, so they asked me to teach in an 8th grade class because national examinations were coming very soon. The 8th graders were very worried about passing the exams because they do not get to go to high school if they do not pass. Even if they do pass, they have to find some way to pay their fees to attend high school, which is about $500 a year. So many of them worry about their future and what they will do next year. I found them well prepared for the exam though and tried to alleviate their worry about passing. I told them their teacher had done a good job, that they were ready, that they should continue to work hard in their studies so they could be good leaders for Kenya in the future.

They wanted to know all kinds of things about America though. Once every 2 weeks they crank up the generator and watch about an hour of television, and they are crazy about WWF Smackdown wrestling. They asked about the wrestler named The Rock. When they found out *"rasslin' is fake"* as we say down south, they were incredulous. There were some disturbing questions though, too. One asked a team member if it is true that all Americans think they are baboons because someone had told them that. They also wanted to know why an African who dies in America is shipped back to Africa for burial in a box labeled cargo, like they have no significance as a person. They asked some very thought provoking questions about some very sensitive issues. What a shame that what little information they get from abroad is something as despicable as Smackdown and racism.

One really good thing that came from our visit to Pehucci though was a win-win for everyone. An unemployed female Maasai doctor came to visit with us at Karina's where we were staying. She was going with us to the Enkasiti Maasai School to teach hygiene and treat some simple ailments of the children. She lived very near Pehucci but had never been there. She asked if we could pick her up on our way to Pehucci since she lived nearby so she could go with us. She was introduced to us as Dr. Cathryn. We did take her with us to Pehucci and got her connected with Miss Lucy. We also told Bishop James Mbai at the tent mission about Dr. Cathryn. The tent mission is another story to come later, but both Miss Lucy and the Bishop said they could hire the doctor for 1 day a week to come work with the children. So Dr. Cathryn now has at least 2 days of employment that she did not have before becoming part of our mission work. It a great success story and one of the best things I think we accomplished.

Our team had a long discussion though about what help is needed in Kenya and how much help. We all agreed that with the Maasai and the other Kenyans that we should not expect to change their way of life to mirror ours. Change in Kenya must come from Kenyans. Yes, we could send the Pehucci children a package of 100 brand new shoes, but what does that accomplish in the long run? Their feet will get blisters that will get infected by the dirt. As they get accustomed to the shoes, their feet will get soft and tender. The shoes will wear out eventually. They wouldn't be able to walk on the dirt and rocks like they can now. So what good would it do them other than needing more shoes when the first ones wear out? Such intervention only leaves them more dependent on outsiders. What we need to do is encourage their faith, encourage their education, fill short term immediate needs that won't leave them dependent, and do some networking of people like Dr. Cathryn, Miss Lucy, and the Bishop, and let the betterment of Kenya come from within. And the people all said.....Amen.

In the footsteps of Pehucci

The Human Dynamo, Miss Lucy with some of her school children

Chapter 4
The Tent Mission
"Robbers at the Door"

I knew when I started these writings that eventually I would have to tell the stories of the 30 street boys at the tent mission in the slum area of Nairobi called Eastleigh (pronounced there as E-sah-lee). I have dreaded coming to this point in the storytelling because the tent mission is the most difficult part of the Great Commission for me to deal with in terms of processing the experience, reflecting on the encounters, and staying practical and real about my abilities and limitations in connection with any changes needed there. Eastleigh is by far the worst slum area of the city, with all that that entails from high crime and corruption to people dead or dying in the street. It is also the epicenter of both the Somali refugee and the Muslim populations of Nairobi. It was the home base of the terrorists who bombed the old U.S. embassy in 1998, killing over 200 people, and it is the place where the most recent group of terrorists were arrested for conspiracy to blow up the new U.S. embassy that opened just before our arrival. So that is our setting for this chapter. Before describing our time there, though, I want to tell you about something that happened at the tent mission about two weeks before we arrived.

Like everyone else in Nairobi, the tent mission adults and children live behind a six-foot fence. Theirs is constructed of sheet metal nailed and tied together. There is a double door iron gate at the entrance, and there was a night watchman. I say *"was"* because he is no longer there because he sneaked off one night to hide and sleep. While he was sleeping, a band of 8-10 robbers came over the fence. People were worshipping in the tent, and the robbers tied them all up, including the 30 street boys who live there. The robbers stole all of their worship equipment: the keyboards, the guitars, the microphones, the speakers, the wires and connectors, everything.

As it happened, the man who runs the mission, Bishop James Mbai, and his assistant named Gideon, were in the offices next to the tent. As is the norm, all doors were locked. In that area, if you unlock a door to go into a room or building, you lock it behind you. The robbers banged on the door and said they were soldiers and that the Bishop was protecting a robber wanted by the police. They told the Bishop to open up, and he did. As soon as the door was opened and the robbers were inside, they said to the Bishop and Gideon, *"We are NOT soldiers. We are robbers."* They then tied up everyone in the offices and began carrying out everything of any value. The Bishop and everyone tied up were put on floor, lying on their stomachs. As the thieves ransacked the four rooms and carried off things, they literally stepped on the backs and legs and heads and shoulders of the people who were lying on the floor tied up, a severe form of intimidation that, in essence, tells the *"captured"* that they are nothing but dirt under the feet of the aggressors. There is a Kenyan way of speaking when describing such ordeals to actually understate the situation and not elaborate in detail too much. When telling us about the robbery, Gideon expressed it by simply saying, *"It was very bad...very bad."* By his soft tone and dropped head, it was painfully obvious how devastated they were to have lost all of their equipment so essential to their expressions of worship. This was, for them, the proverbial boot kick in the gut after one is already on the ground and has had the wind knocked out of him. We asked what had happened with the night watchman. We were told he was never seen again, which was a polite way of saying he most likely was an insider on the robbery.

Prior to our departure for Kenya, our mission leader, Joy Kirschner, had received an email from the Bishop expressing his joy in our coming soon, some very sketchy information about the robbery, and a request that we try to bring them a keyboard if at all possible for their worship services. When we told Gideon we had a keyboard for them, this small, slender, soft-spoken man of God seemed suddenly transformed into a man of might and a warrior for the weak. He was lifted up and vigorous. He cried in joy.

On our first visit there, Gideon informed us that the Bishop had been absent for the past three weeks because he had been very ill and "in hospital." He was that day at home out in the countryside but was still not recovered. It was doubtful we would be seeing him that day, but it was hopeful he would be there Sunday for worship. With that, we set about the work of the day.

As we entered the double iron gate of the Fountain of Life Deliverance Ministries, we were greeted by the biggest smiles we saw anywhere in Kenya, which says much because we were greeted with smiles all the time. As the van entered the compound, little boys seem to come out of the ground. They ranged in age from approximately 6-14. Each one came to greet us and shake hands with us saying, *"Welcome, welcome."* There was much greeting and joy as 30 boys each shook hands with all eight of us. You would have thought there was a political rally going on there was so much *"pressing of the flesh."* This introduction was the most exuberant, delightful, invigorating one we received, I thought. Then suddenly the boys were gone! In a flash, they were gone!

A few minutes later they reappeared with small buckets and were running toward the one, lone water faucet at the compound where they began frantically washing themselves. All of them were dusty from head to toe when we arrived and shook hands. Faces, arms, fingers, hands, knees, elbows, legs, feet, and toes were all covered with a fine powder of dusty dirt. The dust was so thick that their skin looked a whitish gray instead of black. They splashed water from the fountain on their faces; they splashed water from little small plastic pails onto their arms and legs and feet. Then suddenly the boys were gone! In a flash, gone again!

We were left standing there wondering what happened. In a few minutes, we looked up, and coming across the compound were 30 clean, little boys all dressed alike in white tee shirts with an orange band around the collar and sleeves. They were beautiful children before the *"bath"*, but now they FELT beautiful, and it showed in their faces. And it was time to play ball...volleyball and soccer! A team member had brought a badminton set. We used the net from it for the volleyball. The boys were quite good and very fast on their feet. We each had to be on guard though because soccer balls were coming from all directions and you were likely to get nailed by one if you weren't looking!

I spent some time talking with two of the male teachers, who were young men around the ages of 18-21 it seemed. One named Washington was very interested in American things like food and games and living conditions and schools. He was surprised beyond belief to hear that in American we have slum areas in some cities, that we have people living on the streets, that we have a lot of crime in some areas, and drugs are a problem here as well. Like everyone living in the Emerald City of Oz that, in the book, wore special glasses with colored lenses so make the city look green, his view of America was one of all beauty, all riches, and no problems. We had a rather lengthy conversation about the irony of the *"American Dream"* that the more you have, the more you want. The more you have to work, the more you miss out on the really important things in life that matter most. We talked about American education being a free, public education for everyone through 12 grades. He was excited that just recently the new Kenyan government had declared free education for all children through grade 8, but he laughed out loud with great joy and exclamation that in America our children could go through grade 12. He expressed hope that perhaps our educated children would become teachers to help them in Kenya.

Again around lunchtime, suddenly the boys disappeared. Gone, again, in an instant! I was beginning to feel a little like Dorothy in Oz when she says, *"My, people come and go so quickly here!"* What had happened though was that the boys had gone to their "*dorm*" to fetch their bowls and spoons for lunch. Each one has his own bowl and spoon, and it is his responsibility to keep it washed and put away safely so as not to lose it. And the dorm, by the way, is a single room furnished with 5 bunk bed sets, 10 beds total, for 30 boys. Do the math, and picture yourself in a single room with 30 young boys to bed them down for the night, in complete darkness, with only light from flashlights, in the slums of Eastleigh. Robbers had stolen all of their flashlights too, so we sent Julius, our van driver, and Mike, our team member, to go buy some new "*torches*" as they call them, along with a supply of batteries and bulbs.

Since it was lunchtime, just as we had done with the children at Pehucci, we helped serve lunch to the boys at the tent mission. We talked with the cook, Joyce, and visited her "*kitchen*". Her stove was very similar to Mary's at Pehucci, wood burning with a big pot on top. The meal served was corn and beans cooked together. Their corn, however, does not look like ours. Theirs has very large kernels that look like yellow hominy. We asked the cook how long it had been since the boys had had any meat with their meal. She could not recall exactly how long it had been but said, "*I do not believe we have served any meat this year.*" Again, we heard that Kenyan speech pattern of understatement. We were thinking, "*And here it is October and the year almost gone. How could this happen?"* Well, our course of action was clear. Here was a way to make an immediate and positive impact. We all had money for gifts and such, so we just planned to buy fewer souvenirs, pooled some money, and sent our van driver to buy enough meat for the boys to have meat meals over the next two days and for each to have a soda. Getting a Coke or Sprite was a double treat because the drinks came in refundable bottles, which meant they could get money also after the drinks were gone. A soda bottle is worth about 20 shillings, I think, meaning the equivalent of about 25 cents. That amount seems insignificant to us, but to a Kenyan, receiving a refundable bottle is a significant gift.

While lunch was being served, again another surprise *"coming and going"* occurred. The Bishop had gotten word from Gideon that we were there, and he had his wife bring him into the city to see us. We were called into the offices for the usual long protocol meeting of introductions, conversations, discussion, and questions. But the Bishop appeared very, very weak, and it seemed our visit would be rather brief. But as he talked with us about the boys and how the mission is run and how important the tent worship is to the surrounding community, he visibly grew stronger and more robust. We are not sure why James Mbai is called *"the Bishop".* He has not been linked to any particular denomination that we know of that might have a bishop. That title was of little consequence, though, because the boys call him Poppa. He is the one who loves them. He is the one who cares for them. He is their shepherd, the one who fights for their living and their survival day after day. It was unmistakable the love and respect these boys share for their poppa.

They had not seen him in three full weeks, even on Sunday, because he had been too ill to come to the mission. This was a good day for them. We had come to help them, and Poppa had come back to them. Just as the Maasai gave us credit for the good rain that came during our safari trek, the Bishop's return synchronized with our arrival made for a great day of joy and thanksgiving. We were not there the two days they ate meat for the first time this year, but we know there was great feasting and thanksgiving those days as well.

The Sunday we left Kenya, we went to worship that morning with the boys at the tent mission. We met people in the community, from the devastating Eastleigh slums, who come there faithfully to worship each week. We heard the *"joyful noise"* of the singing along with keyboard music and guitar. Worship, again, was somewhat charismatic. Again, we had some difficulty dancing and clapping in church, but the service was indeed Spirit-filled. There were 5 preachers there altogether. The first was a preacher that is there at the mission only on Sundays and whom I did not know.

Nevertheless, I loved his preaching because he was so joyful and active in telling all of us, *"The Lord does not care about your past. He cares about you today, and He cares about your future. There is someone today waiting for you to set him free—free from the past---by giving him the Word. Someone is waiting for you to set him free."* The Bishop was there to preach also, although he needed Gideon's hand to steady himself. And there they stood together, hand in hand, two brothers in Christ, with a common vision of their ministry to street boys to set them free from the ugly life on the streets of E-sah-lee. Yet another preacher was one to whom we were introduced one prior evening and who is nicknamed *"Dancing"* Robinson because his first name is too hard to pronounce. He and his wife Philemon had come out to Karina's where we were staying, and he spoke to us about his work with the Baptist Men's Ministry. His wife is a seamstress who custom-tailored a jacket for me with a lining and cloth-covered buttons. She measured me on Wednesday night, and she brought the jacket to the tent mission on Sunday to deliver to me. The total cost for all fabric and labor was 2,000 shillings (around $25). It was a pleasant surprise to see Dancing Robinson at the tent and even though he did not preach that morning, he was dancing!

Shem Okala was there as the main preacher that day. Shem is the coordinator for all volunteers in Kenya who come through Baptist ministries. He is a very tall, imposing man with a million dollar smile. He had also come out one evening to Karina's to talk with us and share a meal. His wife Ruth was with him that evening. She is a high school teacher who works Monday through Saturday, and every other Sunday. This particular Sunday she was not with him because she was on duty at the school. Shem is a remarkable speaker with a highly amiable command of your attention. His message that morning dealt with reasons not to worry and was based on three different scriptures as proof that God will provide. As it turned out, Miss Lucy and her husband David were at the tent to worship that morning also, and Miss Lucy told us Shem's message was just what she had needed to hear. She had, of late, been feeling depressed and overburdened, and Shem's words rebuilt her spirit to continue her work at Pehucci. This was the same day we delivered the two treadle sewing machines to her as well. So that prayer was answered, and indeed, the Lord does (and did that day) provide. What impressed me most about Shem though was not his sermon that day, but something he had said that night at Karina's. He was talking about how he and others had been spreading the gospel and doing outreach to neighboring countries like Somalia, Tanzania, and Sudan. We asked how, with so little, they could stretch outreach efforts beyond Kenya. His answer was very simple and direct, *"No matter how little you have, you cannot always be receiving. You must give."* It reminded me of the Maasai parents' directive to their Maasai warrior/scholar son, *"You will because you must."* But I was thankful to have met Shem and for the opportunity to have heard him preach. In typical Kenyan understatement style, I will merely say, *"He is gifted."*

No matter how busy the days since my return though, the boys at the tent mission walk daily through my thoughts. I suppose they stay so close to me because they have so much less than even the children of Pehucci. When one compares the two missions, Pehucci seems light years ahead in facilities, dorms, instructional materials, everything. Comparatively speaking, Pehucci is in the Technological Age while the tent mission is still in the Iron Age. Yet, in reality, Pehucci has very little and struggles to stay afloat. The tent mission is often just a meal or two away from having to close the doors. The boys who live there are brave little children surviving in a mean, uncertain world that surrounds them just outside their fence, much like sheep surrounded by wolves. But inside the fence there is Poppa and Gideon and the four dedicated teachers and a cook. In the tent there is safety. In the tent there is peace. In the tent there is singing. In the tent there is hope. In the tent they tell their stories of life on the street in poetry form and dramatization. They say they will never forget the darkness. They will never forget the hunger. They will never forget the loneliness. But loving arms now surround them, and they are not afraid. In Christ is their hope.

I began this chapter with the story of robbers, so it seems fitting to end it with two brief stories of robbers thwarted by goodness. There were the robbers who brutally beat and robbed the man on the road from Jerusalem to Jericho. A Good Samaritan found him and tended him. His life was saved from the streets. He did not die. The Bishop and Gideon are the good Samaritans alive and at work today in the slums of Nairobi, Kenya. They are two men who took to heart the example set by that first Good Samaritan, and they are living out their lives in the most extraordinary of ways by putting the good work into action in a real way in a painfully real world by providing the needed love and care to the street boys of Eastleigh.

The last story may be urban myth in origin, may be true divine intervention. I cannot say for sure. I was not there when it happened. What I can say for sure is that in the tent there is a hole that looks like a heart burned into a low point of the roof. I saw it myself. It is not symmetrical. It is lop-sided. But it still looks like a heart. It is there because one other time robbers had come to the mission and had tried to burn down the tent. They poured gasoline all around it, set it afire, but the tent did not burn...except where the flames burned the heart-shaped hole in the roof of the Fountain of Gospel Tent Mission...and the ministry goes on...

Bwana asifiwe (ah-sah-fee-wee)---The Lord be praised.

Bishop Mbai and Gideon

Tent Mission Boys rescued from the streets

Chapter 5
Maasai Mara

We were to leave the next morning for the safari through Maasailand that would include sleeping overnight in a tent. It was now time to face my biggest fear, bigger even than flying over the ocean, bigger even than being locked up in jail, bigger even than becoming caught up as an innocent bystander in some international incident involving terrorists, bigger even than wrecking out in the van in that crazy Nairobi traffic. My fear was waking up in the tent with a giant python or other constrictor ready to make a meal of me. I have seen pictures of a dissected python that killed and swallowed a man whole. Knowing my fear of snakes, some *"pal"* felt compelled to share that internet photograph with me last year. I haven't forgotten it! And even though I knew Fr. Neel and several others were praying very hard for *"no snakes,"* I must admit that I was not confident that prayers alone would keep the snakes and me apart on the mara (plain). I figured God was too busy with something else to bother with a roadblock to separate one snake and one missioner. But *"oh, ye, of little faith!"* I should have known better. As it turned out, we never encountered a snake of any kind. *"Assante, Christo!!"* (ah-sahn-tay krrrrees-toh---Thank ya, Jesus!)

My other concern was that canvas would be a small deterrent to any hungry lion that had not found a meal recently. Several people had jokingly said to me before my departure, *"I hope you don't get eaten by a lion."* Being eaten by a lion came up in numerous conversations, as a matter of fact, and often enough that the idea became imbedded in my psyche as a real possibility in that setting. So the night before the short plane ride that would take us to Sianna Springs where we would begin the safari, I had some deep, rich, and fervent prayers to send up. The odd thing though is that I have always felt a deep affinity for the Cowardly Lion in the Wizard of Oz, and I can quote more of his movie dialog than any other character's. Now I was living his life and praying for courage; but ironically, it was for courage to face a lion!! The Lord has a mischievous sense of humor indeed!

I have a very dear friend who, in rough times, tells me two things quite frequently. One is, *"You knew the job was dangerous when you took it."* The other is a quote from Shakespeare that says, *"Screw your courage to the sticking post."* I drew heavily on those two bits of Farmerisms and was well prepared to face the adventure ahead when we got ready to board the airplane the next morning. I almost lost all ground I had gained though when I noticed a sign on the side of the aircraft as we were boarding. On the side of the plane, a rectangular area was painted with white dash-like lines and inside the rectangle were the words, *"For emergency exit, cut here."* There was no exclamation point after the word "here" but there should have been!!

Despite the fact that I had forgotten to bring my blowtorch on this trip to Kenya, I got on the plane, but I muttered and grumbled in conversation with the Lord for testing my patience and courage to such extremes. I settled into my seat and maintained my usual decorum under pressure and crisis. I went to sleep--- just like I did when hurricane Camille tore through my hometown of Jackson, Mississippi, when I was a senior in high school. Once I have done all I can do or all that is expected to be done during a pressure situation, I just go to sleep and wake up when it's over.

I did not realize though that this plane ride was just the FIRST leg of the journey. We set down on a dirt airstrip, another first for me. I was standing around wondering what our transportation plan was from that point when I saw another plane, though smaller, coming in to land on that same dirt airstrip. I took a picture of it, but little did I know that the plane coming in was the one we would board for the second leg of the journey that would take us to Siana Springs. Not only had I just landed on a dirt strip, but I was also about to take off from one as well and land on another one somewhere else. I needed another nap!!!

Arriving at the next dirt airstrip, we were greeted by 2 Maasai in traditional dress and 2 others in Westernized clothing. One of these was our driver John. We loaded into an open jeep that comfortably seated all 8 of us plus the driver, and he drove us to the camp compound where we would be quartered for the night. Our safari start time was 3 pm, so we had time to eat lunch and to attend a lecture by a Maasai warrior who has been studying wildlife conversation in the U.S. at a college in California. This is the same Maasai warrior/scholar I told you about in Chapter 2 on the Maasai.

Our safari took us through part of Africa's 200 square mile most famous and best maintained wildlife reserve, Maasai Mara, and it is a phenomenally unique and magical place. The Maasai people, who hold very strong beliefs about the land and the animals, are not people who will hunt game for food. The Mara and the Maasai are in complete harmony with one another, and this is the only place on earth that I know where man and wild animals literally live among each other as neighbors. All through the Mara are small villages with an average population of 10-20 people. Driving through Maasailand, we passed the people out grazing their herds, repairing their mud houses after the big rain, going about their everyday lives among the wild beasts of the plains. When darkness begins to move in on the Mara, it becomes a place that will still the heartbeat and steal the heart. There is a quietness, a calmness, an order to the settling of the day.

Our day on the Mara was one of such enrichment, I still cannot believe I was actually there, that I saw the things I saw with my very own eyes, and heard the things I heard with my own ears. What I experienced there was not a vicarious encounter with nature seen through the telephoto camera lens of some National Geographic special assignment reporter. I was REALLY there – myself – in this unbelievably mysterious and magical earthly kingdom. One has only see it to be confirmed in the faith that the handiwork of the Lord is grand and mighty indeed, and if the Mara can be that soul-stirring and inspirational, what indeed must our heavenly home look like? Greater still, what must the peace of heaven feel like? Thinking back now on the splendor of that day, it does almost reduce me to tears that I was so blessed to have experienced so personally the creative power of God that can blend such contrasts into a seamless weave of life as what can be seen with the Maasai and the beasts in that wilderness known as Maasai Mara.

We had not been out long when rain clouds began to form in the distance. We had found a herd of zebras, a herd of elephants, a herd of Cape buffalo. We had seen a couple of giraffes and numerous small antelopes. Suddenly, our driver John announced to us that lions were nearby, and off the road he goes. We had not gone far when the rain began, and we had to put up the canvas and plastic cover for the top of the jeep. Once the top was on, we had driven a very small way when we came upon a pride of 7-8 lions lying in some brush. John parked the jeep within 20-25 feet of them and shut off the engine. Imagine my surprise at what I thought was pure stupidity on the part of the driver — turning off the engine!!

Then like gnats drawn to a bowl of bananas, suddenly all of these other vehicles arrived and stopped and parked and shut down their engines. The lions were on our left, and 8 or 9 vans had us blocked in with no escape route in the front, back or right. Everyone else was safely ensconced in their enclosed metal boxes on wheels, and there we were, trapped in the middle with a very thin layer of canvas cloth separating us from the fangs and claws of potential death! A gut-wrenching fear gripped me by the throat. It turned my legs to Jell-O, my stomach to pure acid, my lungs to a deflated basketball, my heart to an accordion squeezed shut. The lions lay in brush with the rain pouring down on them, huddled closely together, yawning occasionally and shaking their heads to sling off the water when they became saturated to the point of tolerance. They did not move! Assante, Christo!! Assante, Christo!

We sat there for 20-30 minutes that seemed like a 90-day jail term because even though the lions were just hunkered down in the rain, being boxed in by all the other vehicles felt like being locked up. Finally the rain dwindled to a few drops, and the lions began to move. Thankfully they moved off to the left of where we were sitting in the jeep. We followed them through the brush, but the other vehicles began to scurry in all directions. On the other side of the brush I saw the vans encircling the lions, and once again we were almost encircled with them. I was thinking to myself, "Do these people have no sense about animal behavior?" I am no crackerjack animal behaviorist, but even I know that when you corner a wild animal of any sort and cut off his path of escape, you risk provoking an attack in the animal's attempt to flee. Everyone was just so caught up in the moment of seeing the lions that, I guess, they forgot *"the basics"*.

I, on the other hand, was quite cognizant of the potential problem because (1) I was in the group riding in the open jeep, and (2) I have built my career studying the behavior of the wild beasts known as teenagers! If I have learned nothing else, I have learned you have to *"leave them an out."* I began thinking about all those people back home who had teased me endlessly about getting eaten by a lion. I began thinking, too, *"Man, they are all really going to feel like crap when they go to the memorial service for my tattooed left fibula that is the only part of me to make it back home."* I swear I scare myself sometimes with such silliness! So I just chuckled slightly inside, but I told John I thought we should move to the outer edge of the circle to avoid trouble. Sometimes I am too smart for my own good, too, in thinking I know so much. John really was a phenomenal guide who could *"read"* the animals like looking at a billboard—getting instant information, using it, or discarding it accordingly. But he was good enough to accommodate my wishes, and we moved out opposite some of the vans.

As I soon learned though, John was intent on finding as many lions as possible and getting us as close as possible to them once found. He would be driving along, see an animal far off in the distance, and because of some twitch of an ear or crook of the neck, he would say, *"Lions are there!"* And off we would go, bouncing around in the jeep over ruts and grasslands and small hills, in the direction of yet more lions.

Once the rain fully stopped, there was a brief period of hazy sunlight, and night moved in rather quickly. We continued following the pride of lions as they began gathering around a large waterhole that was about 50 feet across, had a steep embankment that dropped down about 15 feet to the edge of the water, and was surrounded by small dirt mounds that varied in size. The lions gathering at the waterhole for the evening seemed to have assigned seating as each one went to a different mound and there was no dispute about who sat where around the waterhole. There was very little light left when suddenly the most amazing thing happened. The lions began to roar back and forth across the water one at a time. It reminded me of the Dylan Thomas poem *"Rage, rage against the dying of the light...do not go gentle into that good night."*

We have all sat in a movie theater and heard the MGM lion roar in THX and Dolby sound, but as good as the sound quality is for those systems, there is no comparison to being alive at the edge of a waterhole just at night fall in the Maasai Mara. The sound of the roar literally stopped everything — the jeep, the engine, the breath, the heart. Even the molecules of the air seemed to stop stirring. The force of the roar was so powerful, I could actually feel the sound vibrate off my chest. The sensation had such resonance, it felt like the roar went into my mouth, down my throat, and reverberated through my entire body, bouncing from rib to rib. It was the most fearsome sound I have ever heard; it produced the highest level of consciousness I have ever experienced regarding my very own mortality; it was a sound never to be forgotten even in the advanced stages of Alzheimer's. It is a sound that, once inside you, is carried to the end of your days. The roaring had that quality of sound that I have always imagined is what the voice of God must be like. And with that sound, the lions brought down the dark curtain of night.

We raced back to the camp compound for supper after the nightfall experience with the lions, and we settled around a campfire to watch a demonstration of a dozen or so Maasai warriors. The Maasai warriors are a special group. They are the ones that are specially trained to kill any lions that attack the village or the herds. It is their job to track down the lion, hunting it in a group, and each warrior must be strong enough to throw his spear completely through the lion when it is found. Dressed in red that matched the firelight with their skin the color of dark night, the entire dance produced a surreal atmosphere at the camp. Prior to the start of the lion hunt, they prepare their courage by dancing, which is really jumping. It is amazing how high they can jump. Throughout the dance, different members would step out and begin jumping up and down, often jumping 3 to 4 feet in the air from basically a flat-footed stance. The dance and *"music"* itself is quite intimidating. There is no football locker room pre-game hype that can equal the warriors dancing and singing in preparation for the hunt. They have an animal horn they blow. While the jumping is going on, other members sway forward and back. The warriors also make this very deep hum in their throats, and they make this barking type sound deep in their throats. It was not a *"woof"* or *"ruff"* sound, but it was definitely a type of barking noise. The lead dancer was the Maasai scholar who gave the lecture earlier in the day. His job was to blow the kudu horn. The kudu is considered the most beautiful of the antelopes and is quite large in size. The spiral horn of the kudu can be 4-5 feet in length, making it quite difficult to blow and produce sound. Our Maasai scholar was quite adept at it, however. Our demonstration was done at night around an open fire. When worked to the height of the dance, the effect can be genuinely terrifying to Westerners who are not prepared for what they see. I was just glad it was an educational demonstration for us and not the real thing. Scary, scary!

Today the government prohibits the warriors from killing the lions, even if the lion is attacking the herd. The government has promised to pay for replacement of the herd rather than have the lions killed because they are so endangered. So the lion hunt is to become a thing of the past, and while it is important to protect endangered species, it is unfortunate that such an important aspect of Maasai culture will be lost in a few short years. And who knows how long it will take for the government to actually deliver the reimbursement money to the Maasai who lost the herd?

I love studying different cultures and sharing what I learn about them with others, so it is unfortunate that this is one aspect of Maasai culture that a book cannot give you. You have to be there and hear it demonstrated to get the full impact of the fierceness of it all. I have practiced the barking and can do a fairly good imitation, but it just is not the same without the kudu horn and the grunt humming to go with it. And I will never master the jumping!

That night I went to my tent with my head full of questions. *Was I really here? Did I really see the lions? Were they really defying the night?* My nervousness about sleeping in a tent had dissipated a good bit. The camp compound did seem quite secure, all things considered. Plus, it had been a long, emotional day, and exhaustion was taking its toll. The camp automatically shut off the generator for the electricity at 10 pm, so I lit a candle to read a little to unwind. I think it took a whole 5 minutes. Then the candle was put out, and the darkness was the darkest dark I have ever seen. I could actually hold my hand 3 inches from my own nose and not be able to see it. Down south we have a phrase about dark nights when the moonlight is barely visible. We call it *"black dark"*, but even the black dark nights of my Mississippi childhood could not compare to this darkness. It was blind darkness. So I turned over, said a fervent prayer that I would have no night visitors, and fell off the cliff into dreamland.

Around three in the morning, we had a torrential rainstorm, complete with thunder and lightning. My tent mate and I got up, lit a candle, and just listened to the rain beating on the tent roof and heard the wind whipping the tree limbs around. My tent mate was a 19 year old from Colorado, and in the usual fashion of late teens and early adulthood, she did exactly what I would have done at that age at that time at that place. She unzipped the tent and stepped outside under the awning porch to experience the storm more closely. That is when I realized how much I had changed through the years, but how much of me at 19 was still a part of me. After all, it wasn't that long ago that I had gotten out of bed in the middle of the night while on a cruise, taken off my pajamas and redressed myself, just so I could go out on the top deck from 1 am to 2 am just to look at the full moon on that dark and rolling ocean. I just could not go to sleep that night until I had really looked at the moon reflecting on the sea. So rather than grins and grumble that she was opening the tent and exposing us to wind and rain and any animal out there seeking shelter from the storm, I understood what she was doing and why. She stayed out less than 30 seconds, just long enough to gather a weather report that the wind was very high and the rain was very cold, before flopping back into bed. I lay awake another half hour just listening to the storm by candlelight while shadows of the flame skipped around the canvas walls.

The safari continued the next morning around 6 am. Again, John demonstrated his mastery of animal knowledge and was able to show us more giraffes, a lone bull elephant, and another pride of lions. Just prior to finding the lions, we had run upon a half eaten carcass of a rather large animal, identity unknown. John knew the lions were not far away. We found them just as they were finishing up breakfast and getting ready for a morning snooze in the sunshine. One's mouth had a pink stain around her lips and on the white chin whiskers, evidence of a just-finished breakfast. It was here I realized John was either a brilliant guide or a very stupid man because once again he parked the jeep and turned off the engine! Unlike the lions we saw late in the afternoon the day before that were resting and sheltering from the rain, these lions were moving around. One particular lion that was in the brush to the left of the parked jeep got to her feet and began walking toward us with a look of intense curiosity. Several of us began telling John it was time to move, that she was coming too close. He told us, *"Don't look at the cat's eye. Be calm. Stay in the jeep."* Well, I was not about to stay in the jeep if she got in it! One team member who worked several years as a zookeeper reminded us not to run but just to play dead. This lion was now within 10-12 feet of the jeep and much too close for anyone's comfort, except John's, when she simply turned parallel to the jeep and walked around behind it to get to the sunny open spot where a few other lions were already prepared for a morning nap. I may have aged a good 5 years over that encounter, but just to have been there that close was an exhilarating moment, one where again, life or death weighed in. Our presence among the lions was dismissed in favor of a sunny spot on the other side. Whatever the cause, and personally I believe it to be purely divine intervention, we all lived and are alive today to tell this story of how we survived in the lion's den.

As a child I never dreamed of going to foreign places. I loved to study them, and I was fascinated by sounds of their names like Timbuktu, Istanbul, Oslo, Reykjavik, the Serengeti Plains and Mount Kilimanjaro. Never in my wildest dreams though did I ever imagine myself in Africa. But I have been there, and it is now part of who I am. I am one who loves to travel and loves to get outside and interact with the land and nature. Maasai Mara is a place to which one day I am sure I will return. In the interim I have the photographs. I have the life the photographs captured. I have the story written here. I have the dust of the Mara in my nose and lungs. My time on the Mara was worth every anxiety — from the small, twin-engine planes to the dirt airstrips, from the open jeep to the turned-off engine, from the lions to the driver/

guide who is himself a full blood Maasai and true to his heritage of fearlessness among the lions. Like the Maasai who live on the Mara, we, too, have now looked at the lions and spent time in peace among them. For many days now to come, I know when I end the day and turn out the lights, I will recall the Kenya I discovered while working for God. My wages for the work were paid in full at the waterhole, at nightfall, when the lions called down the darkness, and in their voices, the voice of God bounced through my whole being, rib to rib, like a pinball slapped with perfect timing.

Lions on Maasai Mara

Resting after breakfast

Lions gathering around the waterhole for the night – Maasai

Mara Ruler of all on the Mara

Chapter 6
The Cows of the Maasai

I have often said that when I retire, I want to live in a little farmhouse out in the country on a piece of land that has two things: a running creek or river within walking distance of the house where I can fish anytime I hear a catfish calling my name; and two, within eyesight of my front porch swing, I want a farmer's pasture next door where he grazes cattle. I know nothing about tending to cattle. I know nothing about their temperament, their diet, their subtle ways of wiling away the day. I just know I like to watch them grazing on pastureland. So the time I spent in Maasailand was a very restful time for me because I had numerous opportunities to see Maasai herdsmen standing watch over their herds in the grasslands and in the Maasai Mara. Some of the herdsmen were no more than 6 or 7 years old, and we would see them tending as many as 50-100 head of cattle.

Sometimes in our travel from place to place, we saw these young children herding the cows along a major high-traffic highway. Knowing how valuable a single cow is to a Maasai, there being absolutely nothing of greater worth, we remarked several times about how much wealth lay in the hands of those young boys tending such large herds. Indeed, their parents must have trusted them implicitly to have placed such assets in the children's command along with such acute familial responsibility.

Maasai legend and lore says that when God (a deity they called Enkai) created cows, He built a rainbow as a path and sent all the cows down to earth and gave them ALL to the Maasai. In essence, anyone who owns a cow now actually owns property belonging to the Maasai. One of our team members is a cattleman himself. When our Maasai scholar found out that Mike owned so many cattle, he told Mike he would come to America to reclaim them since they all belonged to the Maasai anyway. To have been raised in a rather primitive society, our Maasai scholar had a rather remarkable and sophisticated wit about him, especially when it came to discussing cows in relation to Maasai life.

The Maasai literally build their lives around the needs of their cattle, and nothing takes higher priority than the care of these animals. Consequently, the Maasai have constructed and maintained a culture that has inculcated itself with extensive trainings and rituals, handed down generation to generation, that are designed to ensure the safety, care, and sanctity of the herds. The cows are the life of the community. Through centuries of periodic droughts, when water was scarce or non-existent, the cows kept the people alive because the blood became the water's substitute. Without the herds, death is a certainty for the people and the Maasai way of life. So the Maasai have shunned outside influences for generations in order to perpetuate their tribal identity and their pastoral culture, even to the point of fiercely and viciously warring with other tribes and colonists and stealing their cattle... back. After all, the cows belong to THEM in the first place.

When it comes to the predatory lions, the Maasai have even developed war strategies to battle them and to protect the herd from their marauding skills. Thorn thickets are placed around the herd at night, which is placed in the center of the village so that all may come to the rescue of the herd if need be. Any lion skillful enough to pass the thorn thicket surrounding the village itself and brazen enough to pass through or over the second thorn thicket barricade to attack the herd is certain to find himself in a perilous situation before ever getting the first delectable mouthful of beef. Once discovered, that lion is destined for certain and unmerciful death. Or, shall we say, in the past this was true. Now that the Kenyan government has forbidden the Maasai to hunt and kill lions, even one attacking a herd, the lions now live in relative security. In the past, the lion faced an equally cunning and strong adversary in the Maasai warriors. Certain honors were given to the first and second warriors to strike the lion with the spear and bring him to the ground; but before the hunt was to end, the lion would die at least a dozen deaths as each warrior plunged his spear into the enemy lion.

I had seen a picture once of a group of Maasai warriors standing over a dead lion with no less than 18 spears stuck in the lifeless body. For anyone such as myself who loves wildlife in general, it was a difficult thing to see and a hard thing to forget seeing. I cannot help but admire the power and agility and cunning of lions, and I understand the Maasai's need to kill a marauding lion. I just do not understand the seeming barbarism of overkill. However, once a person has seen first hand the engrossing poverty of the Kenyan life, one then can understand that a single cow lost to a lion is indeed an enormous loss. The detrimental impact that loss has on the family gives rise to an understanding that provides a different perspective that does not excuse overkill but understands it better. I imagine it is a feeling much like an enraged parent that viciously attacks a person or an animal that has hurt their child or invaded their home. Picture JoBeth Williams here in Poltergeist running down the hall screaming, *"Don't hurt my babies!"* You know she would take on any demon from hell to save her child, and that is how a Maasai will defend his cows.

No matter how one looks at it though, the Maasai practice of exchanging cows for girls is something that defies modern day conventional Western mores. In the Kenyan culture, any man wishing to marry must produce a *"bride prize"* for the family. Often, this bride prize is paid in number of cows. The prettier the bride-to-be, the higher the price of the prize. So a really pretty girl might garner as many as 7 cows for the family. Since the Maasai were once a polygamous society, a man with several wives had to pay a good number of cows to get them. In turn, though, if he has several daughters, he is likely to regain the lost wealth as each one marries. Among the Maasai today, polygamy is acceptable. Among Christian Maasai, a man may keep all of his wives if he had them before conversion. Once a Christian, though, if not already married, the man is expected to take only one wife. Getting a wife, whether it is the first or the fifth, requires a *"bride prize"*. Unfortunately, since this marital arrangement is linked to potential financial gains, rarely does the girl have any say about the marriage, and often the girl is given to the oldest man in the village because he is the one most likely to have the most wealth in herds. So young girls of marrying age (starting around 14) are most often married off to older men in their 30's and 40's because they have more cattle for the bride prize than would a younger man. If a man has several wives, there are strict rules about how he must treat the first wife. The man's first wife is chosen for him by his family, but any other wives he may choose himself. So the man may actually love the second or third wife and not the first. He cannot, however, treat the first wife with less regard.

The concept, while it seems so degrading to women and certainly not a practice to be found in a civilized society, truly is no different from the old ways here in America of a young man having to pay a dowry. The Maasai just pay with cattle instead of money. Fortunately, recent governmental changes in Kenya are promoting a change in this tradition. Posters are found in various places that say *"Don't trade girls for cows. Give them education."* No doubt that switch in society will be slow coming, as most cultural changes are. Even if it changed today though, the cows would still remain the predominant financial foundation of the tribal society.

It is that cows=wealth concept that now brings me to a related story concerning the Maasai, their cows, their loving generosity, and the 9-11 tragedy. A young Maasai had been attending college in the U.S. when that fateful day dawned and terrorists left over 3,000 dead and buried in the rubble of the Twin Towers. Although he was a foreigner in this land, he felt like many other Americans that day – that the Homeland was under attack. And he felt the same anger, the same sense of loss of innocence, the same burning tears over the devastation and loss of lives. It was another six months before he returned to his own homeland. There he shared with others the events of that day and horrid details of the sight. The people in his village had not heard about the attacks because of their isolation. When they heard what had happened, they were both appalled at the brutality of the attacks and also empathetic to the losses suffered. Like so many others who wanted to offer comfort and support, the Maasai wanted to do something to help the city of New York. So they gave the only thing of value they had...they decided to give some of their cows to New York. And again, Reader, keep in mind the value of a single cow...and the sacrifice required to give up even one cow...and the Maasai decided to give fifteen. Fifteen cows!!! That is an enormous gift for a people so poor in financial terms, but so rich in generosity of heart. And while some people would say that it was a useless gift, that 15 cows was hardly of any immediate use at that time, I dare say it was as much a sacrifice as any other made to help heal a city and a nation and to comfort thousands of strangers thousands of miles away. The arms of love reach far and wide, and the cows are as much an expression of love as they are an expression of wealth.

So the Maasai and their cows continue to sustain one another and to give each other tranquility and respite.

And I, for one, understand that peace and restfulness that comes from watching cows graze. So for a while longer, I hope the Maasai and the cows will continue to stand apart from the world. I hope they will be able to pass many more days just like days have been passed in the past – one hour at a time, dawn to dusk, standing watch and grazing. How much longer the Maasai can withstand the world influences of terrorism and regional hostilities, who knows? How much longer they can hold on to their cultural lion-killer identities and their pastoral lifestyle, who knows? How much longer can they ignore the modern world encroaching on their land and demanding change? How much longer the Maasai can withstand government pressures to abandon many identifiable tribal traits and customs to advance a more homogenous society in Kenya, who can say? The most likely answer from the Maasai, however, is...until the cows ALL come HOME.

Maasai Cows

Chapter 7
The Power of God in Speed

When I first began writing these travel sections, it seemed important to tell the story of God in Kenya more so than to tell the story of my personal journey with God that took me there. As time has passed, however, since those travels through that African nation, I have grown increasingly aware of the interest people have in how I came upon that road that led to Nairobi and its surrounding villages and towns. I suppose, like me, they wonder how a rough–and–tumble, religiously withdrawn, embedded child of the Deep South who uses a plethora of profanity in daily conversation could have been *"called"* and could have *"heard"* and could have *"answered"*.

In the beginning, I questioned that situation a great deal myself. With many people who get *"makeovers"* – either through plastic surgery or diets or from Oprah's generous wardrobe and hair style do-overs – there are usually *"before and after"* pictures. Some people may be disappointed to discover that my work in Kenya did not significantly change the way I look or behave. I don't have this aura of peace that shines on my face, no halo illumined behind my head, no soft spoken tone in my voice that conveys a godly grace within. I am still fond of and still use favorite four letter vocabulary. I was a decent writer before I went. I am still a decent writer, but not a better writer. So the question begs to be asked: What changed? To understand the answer, though, one must know the full measure of the past – before Kenya. After that, one can draw individual conclusions as to the answer to the question.

To sum up my life *"before Kenya"* into a handful of pages requires a laying open of the soul in almost the same way that a heart patient invites the surgeon to reach in and massage the heart muscle if it should stop in the middle of the operation. Without dwelling on it too much, suffice it to say my childhood was limited in childhood delights, virtually loveless, and fully punctuated by parental pummeling. My adolescence was cagey and defensive. I was dubbed the kid you had to *"whip"* if you wanted to make a reputation for yourself; but in fact, no one succeeded. My attitude was that I had no choice with beatings and belittlement at home, but I did not have to tolerate it from another *"yung'un"*. I concluded that if I could fight well enough to keep a grown man from killing me, I could surely whip any kid on the schoolyard trying to hurt me. So I was completely fearless and confident when it came to my pugilistic skills. What no one knew, though, the deepest secret that I hid, was that I was fearful of everything else. I was extremely shy and withdrawn; I was afraid of the dark; I developed cotton-mouth if I had to talk to people on the telephone. My hands shook uncontrollably if I had to talk to people in person or had to look them in the face. I built massive walls around my heart that both protected me and imprisoned me; and when I went out the gate, I only went beyond those walls in a full fighting charge, prepared to do combat with the whole world if necessary. I was so completely insecure about myself and life that I was still sucking my finger when I left home to go to college. I am ashamed to admit that, but the truth is what the truth is. Long before early adulthood, I had wrecked out in an emotional collision, all tires flat, all windows blown out, roof caved in, doors smashed shut. And I was trapped underneath the crushing steering wheel that was my violent and alcoholic father and my emotionally detached mother trying to survive herself.

Unlike Grandma's favorite vase, whose delicacy is so fragile it requires cabinetry for protection from little hands that could shatter it, breaking the cycle of poverty, violence, and alcohol takes dynamite and sledge hammers. Once I *"escaped,"* I rebuilt the pieces of my life brick by brick, smile by smile, one exorcism at a time.

Today the ghosts rarely ever invade my life, and with the help of many gracious people that God placed on my path, I have been able to build a happy life and even build happiness in others. Even now, though, I still like to sleep with a night light. I'm still comfortable only when I travel with a gun. I have substituted thumb sucking for nail biting. There are still dents in the armor that I have not been able to completely hammer out. Trisha Yearwood said it best in a song she sings: *"These ghosts that haunt me, they get me when they want me, and some days are better than others."* And no doubt right now some of you are asking where God fit into all of it, did I know Jesus then, do I know Him now, did I lean on Him, did I say my prayers, did I have faith in my deliverance? Yes to all, but not in the traditional ways one finds God. Then again, nothing about me has ever been traditional.

The first phase of rebuilding occurred when I was a 13-year old, gangly 80-pounder, and an Air Force Captain who flew fighter jets taught me to drive a huge, powerful piece of black thunder. He was my favorite uncle, and speed and wind were the essential elements of his core. He did not take me out *"riding"* on his motorcycle; he took me out *"driving"*. He put me in control and gave me power, and he taught me that I could impact my own life in ways I never dreamed. That motorcycle became a metaphor for all the things in my life that could hurt me because they were far bigger and more powerful than I.

My driving transformed the machine into a full knowledge that while it looked and felt like I had no control, I, in fact, had all the power I needed to control my level of happiness, my level of success, my level of sheer will and determination. Driving that big, black road machine with the wind now in my blood, not just in my hair and on my face, I tasted real true freedom for the first time in my life, and I decided to pursue it at all costs – never to go back to the oppressive state of being again, no matter how much I would have to fight. Fighting now was no longer what happened to me; it became a means to an end.

I have always believed God put Uncle Byron in my life to teach me to fight with purpose – to win, not just to survive, like he did in those jets. I always believed God put me on that motorcycle with him so I would learn I did not have to stay in the crushed vehicle wrecked in a ditch. There are other ways to travel through Life. I have always believed those driving lessons were God's gift of resilience to me, and it has been that ability to persevere against the odds that made it possible for me to become the life-loving, highly humorous, purpose driven individual that I am. It is that resilience that has made me a leader in my career and has morphed me from shrinking introvert as a child into an adult who has made friends easily and often. I have been blessed with an abundance of love and trust because I have been able to love and trust others despite the fact that I should have turned out suspicious and mean, angry and bitter, cold and crazy.

Along one of those roads, I also found a voice in my pen, and I have always known God put it there. It was a gift given to me early in life; it is still a gift. I may never know all of the reasons God had in calling me to Kenya in October 2003, but I feel certain that part of my purpose was to write these stories and share them. I have tried to imbue each one with a flavor and feel that would propagate in the mind of the Reader so that Kenya would remain, at least to some degree, a part of the Reader's life in the way it infiltrates mine at least once a day.

So you see, God and I have had this ongoing relationship for some time now. He would send me blessings to build me up when violence knocked me down. He found numerous ways to communicate encouragement to me, such as whispering in the wind that ruffled my hair while riding on an open highway. He sought me out and found me in places where I was sure I was hidden and just wanted to stay hidden. He gave me strength of mind and heart to war with the savages in my life, and sometimes one of the savages was my own self. He gave me eyes to see things differently from most people and gave me an intellect that enabled me to paint the word pictures so others could then see what I saw. He made me my own soldier and champion so that I could come home one day from the personal war of poverty and violence. Up until He sent the call to Kenya, however, He had never asked for any favors in return, and when He asked, my first response was not the clear answer Elijah gave saying, *"Here I am, Lord."*

Uncle Byron

Uncle Byron and his motorbike

Chapter 8
Hello, is that You, Yahweh?

Going to Kenya is not something you just wake up one morning thinking about, not usually anyway. Sometimes, though, God has funny ideas about how to accomplish certain things. Look how He handled the situation with Goliath. He gave a kid a rock and said, *"Go get him."* Then there was that butt-kicking Samson gave 1,000 Philistines using nothing by the jawbone of an ass. And let's not forget the time the walls of Jericho came down because Joshua and a bunch of guys were blowing some trumpets. Must have been a hell of a band! Pretty much His calling me to Kenya was about as absurd as each one of those events. But we all know, God has a purpose in all He does, even when He calls the rough and rowdy cussing cowboy types.

The call to Kenya did not come to me on a night wind out on the open range though. It came to me by an email message that popped up on my school address and detailed the mission trip. In the middle of the message was a question printed in large, bold font: *"Is God calling you?"* My first thought was, *"Nope, sure ain't."* Farther down the page was a quote from Jesus: *"Who will go for me? Whom shall I send?"* My second thought was, *"Someone besides me."* As I closed it, though, there was this weird kind of feeling, sort of like the one you get right before you start down that first really big drop on a roller coaster. Usually I delete emails immediately that require no action on my part, but for some unknown reason, I just closed it and left it on the desktop. I remember chuckling to myself, though, and thinking, *"Man, that mission leader would certainly faint with someone like me on her team."* I remember thinking that the Lord would surely laugh, too, over the idea of my becoming a missionary. I could picture the faces of my sisters and closest friends looking at me with total incredulity as I presented the idea to them. I could hear each one individually yet collectively all asking the exact same questions: *"YOU??? Have you lost your damn ....mind???"* They would be saying those last two words very slowly, drawn out for emphasis. And then I could hear them confirming what I was already saying to myself as well: You aren't missionary material. You cuss too much, and that is just one of many reasons why you don't qualify! I decided to just put the idea aside and use it only for *"good humor"* material.

Later that same day as I sat with Frances over a meal at Luigi's, an Italian restaurant near home, I told her about the email and how strange it was that I got it because it came from someone I have never met and never heard of. Her only response was, *"Well, are you going to go?"* I immediately told her, *"Hell, no! I'm not going!"* Then she surprised me even more when she said she thought I should at least consider it, that I should *"seriously"* think about it. After the final decision to go was made, in the many weeks that flowed toward my departure, I know she must have wondered what in the world ever made her say those things. But clearly, I think it was just one more way God chose to communicate some encouragement to me.

The next day at work, I reopened the mail and sent an inquiry to Joy, the mission leader. For the next 7-10 days I communicated feverishly and fitfully with the team leader, asking dozens of questions, collecting information, seeking clarification, pondering preparations, researching destinations, having reservations. I concocted a mixture of both secular and religious reasons NOT to go. I couldn't go because of finances. I couldn't go because I was not spiritual enough. I couldn't go because I had GREAT difficulty talking openly about my faith. I couldn't go because I couldn't miss 10 days of work. There were dozens of reasons why I couldn't go.

As each *"couldn't reason"* was dissolved by various solutions that opened the door to go, I then began to focus my energy developing reasons as to why I did not want to go. I didn't want to go because it was dangerous. I didn't want to go because of snakes. I didn't want to go because of those little, poison dart tree frogs there in Africa. I didn't want to go because I just knew they had funny food I would not like. I didn't want to go because of the filth I was sure to encounter, and my closest friends all know how permanent pressed I like to be. I didn't want to go because I would not be the leader. I didn't want to go because I was afraid to fly over the ocean. I didn't want to go because I did not know anyone else on the team that was going; it would be me and 7 total strangers. I didn't want to go because I didn't want to *"witness"* and openly talk about the Gospel. Religion is very private to me – or at least it was – before Kenya.

So with all those negative reasons I had a list of at least 50 ways to leave Kenya in the dust and keep walking. But again, every reason became insignificant or trivial or easily surmountable. Here is the really weird part though. The main reason I became convinced this was a true call from God to go to Kenya was that every time I began my self-talk about reasons to decline the offer to go, two things would immediately pop into my head and shut everything else out. One was the question Jesus asked, *"Who will go for me? Whom shall I send?"* The other was a song snippet of a favorite hymn of mine which in the second verse says, *"Where streams of living waters flow, my ransomed soul He leadeth..."* It was really kind of eerie because this was a mission affiliated with Living Water International. Without fail though, every single time I tried to argue myself out of going, words of that song would begin flowing through my mind just like a cascade of water, and it would literally dam up all no-go thoughts. Much as I tried to argue, just like Moses argued about going into Egypt, I just couldn't win because of the *"interception"* messages in my head that kept telling me I should be listening to the call. There were times I began thinking I must be having some kind of melt down and was truly going crazy. God could not possibly REALLY be talking to me.

After several days of wrestling over the decision, I very much felt like old Jacob who wrestled with that angel all one night. I had weighed in all angles of the issue; I had body slammed the idea several times. I threw upper cuts and round house blows to knock it down. I jabbed at the midsection; I kicked the kneecaps; I even threw a rabbit punch or two in my effort to win the rounds. But despite all my attempts, I lost ground daily and was crying everyday – because I KNEW what the answer was. I KNEW what God was asking of me. I

KNEW I could not escape this journey, and I just did not want to go. I was that child again – looking for safety, looking for comfort, looking for security, and I just did not want to trade my now *"pretty life"* for the ugliness of danger and poverty again. And I cried because I was ashamed of my initial answer to God. How could I show such ingratitude when He had done so much for me and had never asked anything of me before? Now here He was asking for the first time, and I was telling Him no. And here He was, turning to me to get a job done, and I was fighting him at every turn.

Finally, after what seemed like forever to me, but just a very short couple of weeks for Joy, I was absolutely exhausted from arguing with God about it. So I sat down one evening and wrote Joy an email that said in so many words:

> *I have no idea why God wants me to go with you to Kenya. I am not your typical mission type person, but I am tired of wrestling with God over this situation. So I going to stop questioning, and I am just going to "cowboy up" and go on pure, blind faith.*

It was the most liberating decision! I felt right about it. If analyzed too closely though, basically it boiled down to the fact that God just wore me out. I didn't feel too badly about that though after a friend pointed out to me that He did the same thing with Moses when he kept making excuses not to go to Egypt. That was the pivotal moment I knew I wasn't crazy — because as that decision was set, all anxiety and fear was released, and there was a Great Peace about my destination and my Destiny. With the words, *"I will go,"* the stomach acid stopped churning. The chronic headache went away. I was washed with a sense of full fledged freedom again – like the first time I drove *"The Motorcycle"*. God had a plan for me, one that would require me to burst out of insulated comfort. There was an adventure down the road, a broad and bold adventure. All I needed to get me there was the will to obey God and the courage to ride an open road again. That road would lead me across the ocean into an unknown land among a nation of strangers, in the company of strangers, for some strange reason unknown to me. And it was ALL ok. I didn't need a burning bush to tell me it was the right decision.

Chapter 9
The Devil in the Mix

One would think that preparing for a life-altering journey would require innumerable details and untold hours of planning and packing, parceling and piling and pressurizing, as well as just plain having a whole bunch of stuff to do. Oddly enough though, so many of the detailed aspects came with ease.

I had two trunks weighing the airline limit of 70 pounds each, and each one was filled to capacity with books, clothes, school and medical supplies, and a sundry of other things. My 140 pounds of give-away stuff poured in like a flash flood that fills the underpasses of the concrete canyon near downtown Dallas in April. Strangely, though, I did not have to ask for a single donation. People heard I was going to Kenya, and their hearts took action. All I had to do was *"pack tight"*.

When it came to the financial aspects of the trip, expenses rapidly accumulated well above the original price quote because I was not the least bit prepared for overseas travel. I had never traveled abroad other than a couple of cruises to Grand Cayman and Cozumel; so I have no passport, and I needed one ASAP. Expediting the passport increased its price to almost double the usual cost. Also I had not had any foreign travel immunizations. I was able to get a couple of shots at the health department, but the majority of the shots had to come from elsewhere. By the time I finished getting all the shots, I had been immunized against everything from tetanus to typhoid, hepatitis to yellow fever, and everything in between. The final tally was nine shots at the cost of over $700, and I still have malaria pills to take.

One thing I learned before leaving is that when God decides it is time for you to travel, He doesn't plan economy packages. BUT he does provide provisions, and not one dime of the expense came from my pocket except for my personal spending money. Every penny of the expense came from very generous and God-loving people who wanted to play a part in sharing the Good News with the good people of Kenya. Donations ranged from $5 to $2,000, and I never had to spend one minute worrying about *"where the money would come from."* I found out not only is God a computer geek sending out emails to notify missioners when it is time for them to journey out, but he is also a good financial planner as well. Whoever said the devil is in the details got it all backwards.

Never doubt though that the devil was lurking in the shadows, waiting for his chance to enter the picture. Indeed he jumped in practically from the very beginning. He came handing out doubts like a dark horse candidate handing out leaflets on election day. He chipped away at my *"right decision confidence"* like a woodpecker drilling a hole in my resolve. He wanted me to fail. He wanted me to turn back. He wanted me to be afraid. He succeeded only in planting the fear. Knowing how much of my life had been spent in fear, old Beelzebub thought the fear would be great enough to change my mind and change my direction. Knowing how I have always responded to fear since childhood, that I always came out swinging, he should have known better. But he did not know my heart and mind like God did, so he was wrong in thinking fear would be an influential force strong enough alone to make me shrink from the challenges and run to safety.

My fight against the implanted fear was an enormous challenge and one that was completely unexpected. But strange things began to happen just a couple of weeks after making the final decision to go, things that had never happened before. It all started out simply enough with joking friends telling me they hoped I did not get eaten by a lion. This demise was mentioned to me on dozens of occasions. Then I began getting emails about life insurance which I had never received before (or since for that matter), and they asked the question, *"What will your family do if you die?"* Then news came about the robbery at the tent mission we were scheduled to visit. During all these months, too, the U. S. Embassy in Nairobi had been closed since June because of terrorist threats to bomb the new embassy. You may recall that the old embassy had been leveled by a bomb blast back in 1998, killing over 200 people. Many people were telling me, *"I can't believe you are going over there when airline travel is so dangerous in and of itself."* The 9/11 fear was still impacting travel decisions for many. So the closer time drew toward departure, the more intense the fear became that I was headed straight into a hell I might not get out of.

The fear being generated by the Old Impostor evidently was not directed solely at me either. Some of my closest friends began to have deeply rooted fears for my safety on the trip. Some were even having nightmares about it. *"It is just a feeling,"* they would say. *"I just don't feel good about it."* On the surface I tried to assure them everything would be fine; but inside my own mind, the fear gripped me to the core and just shredded my guts the way a bull does when he gores a man to death. It was the most intense fear I have ever known — the thought that I would go and not come back home. As I told Fr. Neel, I was not so much afraid of dying or dying young; I just did not want to die in Kenya.

Now I am not one who will readily admit fear of anything, but I became so convinced that I had a true and legitimate reason to be afraid that I HAD to talk to someone. I needed to get my ducks in a row...just in case. I told a very small number of people whom I counted on to take care of various things in the event that I did not return alive. I lined up things and settled affairs. I talked with Fr. Neel about funeral arrangements and music. I put together a packet of vital paperwork like power of attorney, a copy of my passport, a list of key contacts. I had pictures made of family and friends and pets to take along with me, hoping for some last minute comfort from those faces and whiskers should my end not come instantaneously. I gathered some of my favorite photos to take along with me also. I can't say that I lived each day to the fullest at this point before I left. Had I done that, people would surely have grown suspicious. It would be unlike me to skip work and go fishing, or to skip work and just stay home playing my favorite music and dancing around the living room with a dog in arms. As much as possible I tried to carry on my regular routines because I did not want my closest family members and friends to worry.

I think I did a really good job of keeping the fear an unknown element with most of the people around me.

Aside from the four or five I had to tell because I needed them to handle certain things, I don't think anyone had even the remotest clue as to the inner turmoil that was beating the crap out of me daily. Before leaving though, I became thoroughly convinced that something bad was going to happen — a lion or a terrorist — a robber or a mob — something terrible that I would have no control over. I thought of Jesus in Gethsemane just hours before his arrest, knowing his fate, knowing the danger, knowing the death that awaited Him. I asked myself if perhaps in this process of preparing myself to do what I was sure God intended me to do, had I become a bit mentally deranged? Was this whole mission thing some delusional journey I was to take, and was I experiencing some mental illness characterized by a Jesus complex? It was all very scary stuff either way I looked at it, very scary, whether I was sane or not.

One friend told me that I did not have to go if I was so certain some bad ending stood on the other side of the world waiting to choke the life out of me. One friend told me that no one would think less of me if I changed my mind and decided not to go. One friend said, *"No doubt it is dangerous. But then, getting in your car each day is dangerous, too."* Then I thought of Frances's favorite phrase that she likes to use with me whenever I complain too much about simple or silly things being too hard. She will look me straight in the face and say, *"You knew the job was dangerous when you took it."* I always smile when I hear her say that because she is so honest and true in keeping me *"real"* about so many things in my job, in my family, in the church, and with life in general. Old Hickory did not smile though because he knew every time I heard that, I shut up whining and complaining and tackled the problem with renewed vitality and strength. The devil was losing his grip. He had me filled to the brim with fear, but he could not get me to spill over the edge and tell God, *"Nope. I'm not going. I know I said I would, but I have changed my mind."*

Many faithful Readers are now probably sincerely asking the question, *"Well, why were you so scared? Didn't you trust the Lord to take care of you?"* All I can say is that those words make a very nice platitude unless you are the one frightened out of your wits. After all, recent world news reported some missioners killed just within the past week. Missioners are killed around the world just like indigenous people are when their paths cross marauding rebels or politically motivated insurgents with an agenda that does not include loving the neighbors or the visitors. But yes, I prayed for strength to face whatever lay ahead in the journey. I asked for safety for the team. But God knows I am a worrier and a do-er. I can put things in His hands and not worry so much about myself after that so much as I worry about the others involved. What about my loved ones and family?

So once again it was time to just stop questioning and *"cowboy up"* again. I had never once considered backing out after the decision was made to go to Kenya. Even on the longest night with the greatest number of tears, it never crossed my mind to back out. Nor did I ask, *"Why, Lord?"* I remarked to a chosen few who knew the fear that I just could not believe God would bring me through so much ugliness in life just to send me off to some foreign country to do me in. Hell, He could take me anytime He wanted right here from Forney, Texas. He didn't have to send me to Kenya to do it.

Once I make a decision though, it is a rare thing for me to change my mind; so backing out was never an option. Just as I decided initially to go, I decided at this point that *"This Plan"* was not mine to question. If my not coming back alive was part of the plan, I had to trust that there was some full and meaningful purpose behind it and that purpose was not for me to know right now. With that resolve, to go to Kenya even with the pile of fears bundled up inside me like a mound of dirty laundry, I left these United States fully aware of my fear and fully aware that I was truly in God's hands — completely. It was a very uncomfortable feeling. Several friends will be shocked by that statement, but I am so accustomed to being in charge that literally putting all control in His hands was sure to feel like the one on the end of a coiled barbed wire when the person on the other end lets go. It was sure to hurt. Becoming a backseat passenger rather than a front seat driver just wasn't my style. I do occasionally like to *"Let go and let God"* as they say; I just don't like to do it often. I think He expects us to expend some effort. God understands that about me, as He understands all things. He did not hold it against me, nor did He turn loose of the other end of that coiled barbed wire.

The devil is another story. He is STILL pissed off.

Chapter 10
A Blessing Wall

It would be impossible to write about my Kenyan experiences without spending a great deal of time talking about the friends, new and old, whose impact so significantly enhanced my growth all along the path to Kenya and back. Each one would be highly embarrassed, I am sure, if I identified each by name. They are all very humble and modest people (unlike the writer friend they share). Many of these friends know one another or at least know OF each other but may have never met. Some have been with me for years, decades even. Some I met for the very first time as I made my way in and around Nairobi and Maasailand. Each had his or her own way of traveling with me; but indeed, all traveled and all took at least a vicarious journey, if not a symbolic one. My trip would never have been as meaningful as it was had it not been for their inclusion on the trip. Rather than *"changing the names to protect the innocent"* — they will simply remain anonymous, and you, the Reader, are left to your own designs to pick a name for them or try to guess who's who. Whichever you choose, my point here is to convey my deepest affection for them all. The Lord blessed me abundantly when He gave each of them to me as a present, and they fill me with joy beyond measure each day.

I got on an airplane in Dallas, another in Houston, another in Amsterdam, before I arrived in Nairobi late one evening in October. I rode many miles in a van all through the streets and outskirts of Nairobi. I walked and played among groups of children. I saw animals in the wild. I rode planes that landed on dirt airstrips. I met dozens and dozens of people in Kenya. After several days, I boarded a plane out of Nairobi back to Amsterdam, another back to Houston, another back to Dallas. I calculate that I traveled over 21,000 miles when all was said and done. That was quite a trip for someone who has only a gypsy spirit but not one ounce of gypsy blood in them. During each mile that passed, each minute that passed, everywhere I went, every step I took, I carried three very personal items in my right pocket...always.

One item is a silver James Avery pendant that is shaped like a shield. It can be put on a chain and worn as a necklace or put on a key ring. I carried mine on a key ring. It has an Episcopal cross on one side, and on the reverse is a dove. Imprinted above the dove are the words, *"Fear Not For I Am With You."* It was a Christmas present I received 10 months before my journey began, and it had always given me such *"shoring up"* in rough times that I could not imagine going without it. It is one of my most cherished possessions.

The second thing I carried with me everywhere I went was a small silver crucifix given to me the night before I left for Kenya. It has the word *"Bethlehem"* engraved on the back. The friend who gave it to me had had a good friend who was murdered a few years back. That friend of his had bought the crucifix when the two of them had traveled to Bethlehem one year. It was the only thing my friend had that was connected to his lost friend. Giving it to me for my trip made it one of the most unselfish gifts I have ever received.

The third thing I took with me everywhere was a single key – the one to my own front door, to remind me of everything about my home and the safe harbor it provides. I count my home as one of my greatest blessings; because even though it is nothing large or fancy, just a simple brick house, no matter how bad or rough a day can be, I have a home when many do not. To me, that home is a place of rest from any hard travel, where little *"puppers"* always greet me and kiss me with great enthusiasm, and where I can always find my very best friend sitting on the back porch in mild weather or by the living room fireplace when it grows more harsh.

That front door key might as well have been a tiny microchip for all the information it carried. Every treasure in my home was contained in that small piece of metal: my walking canes and all the places they represent, my favorite books in the study, the pictures of my family, the squeaky toys for the little pup, the feather pillow that my grandmother made that I still sleep on, and literally hundreds of other memories and treasures. Each day those three small, simple tokens of love and friendship gave me a peace that helped me focus on the work at hand. They brought me pure comfort in uncertain times because it was like having those friends there with me all the time, like 3 guardian angels.

When I packed my one carry-on, I made sure to pack a large envelope filled with 10 greeting cards. Each one was sealed in its own envelope and contained a special message to be read at the end of each day in Kenya. The friend who put this packet together even built each message around a baseball theme, a card for each of the 9 innings, because she has heard me preach enough sermons about the merits of baseball and its correlations to life. Each card offered words of encouragement for the work done that day based on the team itinerary that I had distributed to family and closest friends. Those cards were like getting mail. With the advent of email, many people do not remember or have never known the sheer thrill of getting a letter in the mail from family or a friend when you are far, far away from home at summer music camp or vacationing out in the country at grandma's house. It is a reconnection with home, and it is vital in reenergizing one to tackle one more day away from home to finish some hard or enriching work far from home. One other thing that same friend did for me was to give me what I call my *"journey song"*, a powerful song that so clearly expressed everything I felt and everything I needed to say...

"It's hard to take the first step when I don't know the way; each turn is so uncertain. I've learned to walk by faith. But You gave me a promise that You would never leave, that You would lead and guide me, and Lord, I do believe. Lead me, Lord, and I will follow. Lead me, Lord, and I will go. You have called me; I will answer. Lead me, Lord, I will go." When a friend knows you well enough to know you needed that song, they must be a friend with great insight and spirituality.

At my church there is an intercessory prayer group called the Vine and Branches. Members of that group received a list of team members and prayed for the team before and during the trip. Each member of the prayer group also took a single team member's name so they could pray for that individual. I have no idea which Vine and Branches member had my name. They remain anonymous to me even to this day, but the prayers of that friend were certainly meaningful and regarded with great thankfulness. After all, I saw no snakes. I did not get eaten by a lion although I was close enough to have become breakfast. I did not get sick from the food or water. I was energized every day for fresh work in sharing the Good News with the strangers all around me.

In addition to this group, there is another group I call my prayer warriors. They are a large and varied group of friends who are vehement and avid prayers (as in prayers, a noun) who daily held the equivalent of board meetings with God. Their primary goal was to pray for the team's protection; so daily, sometimes several times daily, they lifted us all up in prayer. The number of warriors was large. I don't know exactly how many there were because each of those friends had other friends they invited into the war council, so to speak. Whatever the number, though, they are special people with inroads to heaven, I am certain; and their faithfulness in prayer, I am convinced, is what brought me home.

This large prayer group was divided into smaller segments, and one segment had an unofficial leader of that group who for years has been my most avid supporter and biggest fan. In whatever I did, I could always count on her strength and assistance even though she often seems like some bee that zooms past your head, never even seeing you, because she is doing fifteen things at once. She never fails to surprise me with her zaniness, yet she has this unwavering solidity of faith unlike any other Christian I have ever known. She is as rock solid as that stone that was rolled away from the tomb that Easter morn. But she can sometimes be a pill, too; and when she sets her mind to something, it is hard to tell her no. So I figured if I had her praying for me, I would surely come home in one piece, if for no other reason than that God would simply acquiesce and say, *"Ok, ok, I'll ensure the trip if you will just sit still for a minute and stop talking!"* I am still waiting, though, for those special mission boxer shorts she promised me as a gift that say, *"Bless me today, Lord."*

I have spent almost 30 years in education as a teacher and an administrator, so I am well aware that often we impact others in ways we can never imagine and ways in which we are totally unaware. We rarely get the feedback that tells us how influential we have been in helping some child or young adult reach a life long dream. Likewise, there were three friends I met in Kenya who have no idea what a significant impact they had on me, but they set a model for me that may be only an aspiration, but it is an ideal framework worthy to pursue in building all our lives.

One is a preacher who had such acute insight into my own thoughts and feelings that I almost believed he was reading his text from some invisible screen on my forehead. He opened his Bible study with us by telling us about a man who said to Paul, *"Come over to Macedonia and help us."* He compared Kenya's need for help to that of Macedonia and our coming to that of Paul. His vision of what it took for us to get there had clarity like that of a prismed glass; he saw all facets of it, and his words mirrored every emotion connected to our travel and work. He touched my heart so tenderly with his thanksgivings for our having come to share the Good News with them. It felt like a blind man recognizing a friend, like he ran his finger along the wall of my heart to discover me, like a child runs a stick along a picket fence just for the discovery of a clattering sound. His words so closely aligned with my heart that even though he probably would not remember me at all if I returned to Kenya, I would know him as someone who knows me well enough inside to be my twin.

The other friend is a very soft spoken man with a great love for children. There is a peace about him that settles on those around him as he goes about his business in a most unassuming way, just quietly doing the work of the Lord for the children of God who have been abandoned on the streets. The burdens of his job are loaded with danger and heavy with responsibility. He does not falter though. He does not waver in his commitment. He does not bemoan how much he must do with so little that he has. To look at him you would never think that small, thin man could move mountains, but he does so daily. This Quiet Man moves mountains of poverty, mountains of shame, mountains of sorrow, mountains of pain; and he replaces each one with a row of hope, a row of love, a row of independence as he tills a green valley called Kenya Tomorrow.

The third friend is a doctor who lives hand to mouth, regularly not knowing where or when her next meal will come, because she is a doctor who cannot find paid employment. I cannot imagine what it must have taken for her to have achieved all that she has in the face of such odds. It is rare for a woman in Kenya to get even a high school education, let alone a college education and medical schooling; and these things did not come to her because she was one of the lucky ones who grew up in a family of wealth and privilege. Even more amazing than her educational achievements though is her daily living. Even though she is chronically unemployed, she goes to work every single day — to clinics, to hospitals, to schools, to missions — to offer her skills as a physician. She knows they cannot pay her, but she says that her job as a physician is to help others whether she is paid or not. At best, at the end of a work day, she may receive a little food for her services; but if not, she will still go to work again the next day. She will rise at dawn and begin walking, going wherever the Lord leads her, wherever another needs help. In the late evening, she will walk back home along the same red, dusty footpath of the morning, having served others in the model of Christ.

Her love for the Lord compels her to give such comfort to others, even in the face of her own discomfort that includes the same hunger felt by thousands.

Then there are the two married couples whose influence has changed almost everything about my personal and spiritual life. Seeing them and spending time with them has given me a renewed sense of the meaning of the word *"connection"*. They connected with me in an instrumental way that made my trip to Kenya possible. They have stood in for me during my absence at times, and they have stood up for me when I had to stand in silence. Whenever I asked for help, they gave all. They are now the model I follow when building my new connecting roads to others or when making repairs in my old roads back home. They are the concrete and mortar, the rebar and steel beams, the quality assurance that the bridges will not fall and the foundation will not crack. Their coming into my life has made all the difference in what I did in Kenya, what I do now, and what I will do in the future.

A couple of years ago when I turned 50, I had this great birthday party at the Ballpark in Arlington. I was lucky enough to find 50 people willing to come out in public and admit knowing me. It was without doubt one of the best parties I have ever had or ever attended. It ranks in the top 3 happiest days of my life. While the point of finding 50 friends to come to the Ballpark was to commemorate the 50 years, one friend for each year of my life, it also gave me an incredibly real visualization of just how blessed I am to have so many friends. The friends I have mentioned in this chapter are by no means the only ones who impact my life in wonderful and amazing ways on a regular basis. There are dozens of you. Those mentioned here in this chapter and all of you others are listed below by initials. I built it like brick blessing wall, as my physical picture of every one I consider a dear and influential friend. Some friends have the same initials, so even though it looks like I duplicated some, I have not. Each set of initials represents one individual. This blessing wall is my simple way of giving you a physical look at the highest regard, the deepest affection, and the utmost respect I bear for each of you. The last block contains all letters and represents anyone inadvertently omitted. Let's face it; your friend here is past 50, and forgetfulness is one of the first signs of aging. The empty block next to the last one is there for the next new friend I meet. So check the wall and find yourself there. I counted you somewhere, and I asked the Lord to give you a special blessing because you have given so many to me.

FF	KK	VM	KP	AB	MM	JT	GM	JC	PB	LM	LC	MA	JA	DN
SN	LB	DE	RK	JK	DE	JE	PE	DS	KH	BT	RL	GA	DA	VB
BW	DC	DC	SY	JV	BP	DV	CM	JT	VD	BB	PO	CO	MB	NB
JK	AK	SM	CT	FA	MH	MF	RP	KC	VG	CG	VK	DK	RF	CR
PB	JB	DW	IW	SA	JB	KJ	RW	DB	JV	SC	TC	SE	MB	KB
RG	CH	JJ	KK	NM	SM	AW	KR	HR	LM	RH	MH	CN	BP	JS
FS	ST	SW	SG	CG	RW	PW	SH	PT	VL	CW	LN	JM	SO	BB
RM	BB	CS	MS	SC	TC	LW	MG	AC	SC	DF	GJ	CH	CS	ML
SL	MM	TM	EM	JM	PN	JN	PP	JR	JR	DR	LR	LS	DS	JS
SW	BW	SB	GP	VM	DV	EJ	GL	TC	CS	LW	BP	CA	MH	KK
LL	RG	RJ	JP	KR	JW	MV	JC	CD	VT	TW	CS	DB	LP	JP
JB	DB	LC	KM	TH	JB	KC	LC	DE	MH	BH	JJ	KR	MM	FT
JM	LW	LA	BM	AP	DB	RW	BH	NB	AS	AW	NH	JD	DW	DH
KP	JP	MB	RW	GW	CM	BM	KP	AW	CW	BM	JM	EM	JM	EB
ST	MR	WW	MC	AH	LM	DS	OW	EH	RC	JC				A-Z

Chapter 11
Stones, Rocks, and Pebbles

Note to anyone younger than 40 or older than 65—If you do not know the songs mentioned in this chapter, it would be well worth your time to find them, hear them, burn them into your memory, and return to them in quiet times of reflection.

Long ago when I was a teenager and knew everything, I had no qualms about bestowing upon Simon and Garfunkel the respective titles of our nation's greatest modern day poet and the nation's most talented vocalist, not only for our time but for many decades past as well. The songs written by Paul Simon were as lyrical as you could get this side of heaven, and the voice of Art Garfunkel gave those lyrics a life they would never have lived had they been sung from the lips of some other performer. Their songs spoke very intimately to a generation of us who, at that time, so often felt disenfranchised, lost, alone, and bewildered because we were living in a world that appeared to be coming apart at the seams before our very own eyes.

Our nation was strongly divided on our military's presence and expansion in Vietnam, as well as our government's apparent lack of commitment to get in, get it done, and get out. With the demolition of segregation and the broadening of civil rights, we saw once civil men, both black and white, prompted to violence and fighting in the streets. My high school was even occupied by police in riot gear due to racial unrest. Leaders and change makers were being assassinated in displays of public carnage never before seen in our democratic society. Men were walking on the moon, but student unrest on college campuses escalated to the point of their occupation by national guardsmen. In today's world the idea of using the military as peacekeepers does not seem like such an oxymoron; but in the late 60's and early 70's, it was as foreign a concept as perestroika and an insane idea that catapulted some peacekeepers into the mélange that led to the deaths of unarmed college students at Kent State in Ohio. Two weeks later police shot up a dormitory at Jackson State University in Mississippi, just across town from where I lived. But above all this clamor and calamity, this death, destruction and mayhem, there were the songs of Simon and Garfunkel, whispered into the dim recesses where we retreated to think, to lick our wounds, and to sort out the mess we were all making of our lives and our way of life.

"Hello, Darkness, my old friend, I've come to talk with you again..."
     – The Sound of Silence

"When you're weary, feeling small..."
     – Bridge Over Troubled Water

"All my words come back to me in shades of mediocrity..."
     – Homeward Bound

"Time it was, and what a time it was, a time of innocence, a time of confidences..."
     – Bookends

"Where have you gone, Joe DiMaggio, our nation turns its lonely eyes to you..."
     – Mrs. Robinson

"The future is now, and it's time to take a stand so the lost bells of freedom can ring out in my land."
     – A Church Is Burning

"The mirror on my wall casts an image dark and small, and I'm not sure at all it's my reflection."
     – Flowers Never Bend with the
       Rainfall

"Thinking it over, I've been sad. Thinking it over, I'd be more than glad to change my ways for the asking."
     – A Song for the Asking

Yes, we were as dark and brooding as any other previous generation of teenagers who believed all adults, especially our parents, were wrecking the world and that we were destined to inherit nothing more than a big, huge, gigantic piece of crap. Simon and Garfunkel were there to soften our edges; and when we were worn out on angry energy expended with Led Zepplin and Steppenwolf, songs like *"For Emily, Whenever I May Find Her"* would fill in the silence and remind us there was still some poetry in the world.

  Some of us were quite hardened though, and I was one like that. By my senior year of high school, I had gone through half dozen infatuations and two volatile love affairs, both equally tragic and both wounding to the core. So I took great solace anytime I heard the empathetic and consoling words of the tune *"I Am a Rock."* I had destined myself to be just that – *"a fortress, deep and mighty."* I understood in very personal terms the raw essence of the words, *"A rock feels no pain and an island never cries."* I was wreckage as a child; but in high school, I became a rock. When young, if I had understood it to be possible, I would have chosen to be a rock then; but I was too young, too innocent and trusting to be guarded, withdrawn, and reserved. But being a morose teenager who had been hurt way too much and way too often physically, after only two failed love affairs, I decided the emotional pain was far worse. So I abandoned the idea of finding happiness in love. There was only me, and I had to take care of Me. So there I stood among my peers, a rock of resistance, a boulder of badness with brains. Back then brainy kids never had troubled souls and never had a chip on their shoulders. But there I was, and I was not one to be ignored.

Until I made this trip to Kenya, though, I thought I was still a rock. Many people have said they see me as a rock as well; but it is a good rock, a solid rock, a *"Rock of Gibraltar"* kind of rock. I take pride in that compliment. I like being that kind of rock for others, steadfast and true. It is so much better than being the kind of rock I was when I was young and angry and mourning quietly with Paul Simon poetry. Then I was like some sharp, giant monolith sticking up out of the desert, defiant and challenging. Now I was a rock people could climb on and hang onto and trust my solidity. I was a rock strong enough to stand and turn full face into a storm while others took shelter behind me. I was a rock with purpose and a meaning beyond mere defiance of cruelty. As an adult, I liked the rock I had become.

But just as God has always done, He made different plans for me and helped me discover them. I was not destined to be a rock forever, but only for the time it served His purpose for me to be one. During my self evaluation and life reflection in deciding whether Kenya should become a piece of my life, God and life worked on me to mold and shape me down into a smooth, round pebble. There are no more sharp, jagged and ragged edges, except on a rare occasion when a sword-wielding warrior angel is needed to combat some injustice. Then my alter ego takes over, and I once again turn razored and caustic. But for the most part I am like those stones in the river that have been washed and washed and washed over and over by the moving, loving hands of the water who knows the stone is to become something else. God has poured water over me time and again, when I have been blistered by the meanness of others, when I have been withered by losses, when I have been thirsty for change, when I have been dried out beyond tears, when I have been hot with anger and in need of cooling words.

Even after I came back from that African excursion, after all the smoking garbage heaps and dusty poverty, I just knew I was still a rock. Only a rock could have defied the devil in his wily plans. Only a rock could look at the ugliness of starvation and filthy shanties and still see a beautiful country filled with beautiful people. Only a rock could maintain its self composure when a lion rose to its feet, ambled forward, and stared with curiosity at the invaders of its wild morning. Only a rock could hug the children of Kenya and leave them behind. Only a rock could withstand the heartbreak of a child wanting more education when no financial opportunity existed to make that happen. Only a rock could vividly and repeatedly relive all of the events in order to tell all of these stories.

Somewhere in the process though of recounting the experiences and visualizing all the faces again, I discovered my new path, the new road the Lord has set me on. I am amazed, amazed beyond imagination, that these stories have been so influential in the lives of so many people. The people in Kenya in these stories are not the only ones who have felt the vibration of the storytelling. These stories have been sent regularly to a group of about 70 people. Those 70 have shared them with several friends and relatives who are complete strangers to me. These kindred strangers, though, have in turn also shared the stories among even more extended familial groups and social circles, and the circle widened

133

with each sharing. So in that regard I have come to realize I am no longer some rock in the middle of a river that the water rushes around. I have become a pebble dropped in the water of a smooth lake, and the ripples of my presence spread out wider and wider in the course of God's plan. That smooth lake is our lives here in a land of freedom, where we enjoy so many comforts and the sheer peace of sitting on our back porches during sunset watching barn swallows raise little families this spring. We have the green grass of home. We have the cold, clear water to slake our thirst, literally and spiritually. We live our lives in relative ease.

While ripples in the water create great symbolism for the reaching out and spreading out of good things, it nevertheless also represents a disturbance of the norm. Being a risk taker and a change maker, as is my usual custom of shaking things up periodically, I have jumped into the water of our smooth lives to cause a few ripples. We have always heard about the *"circle of life"* and that pattern to be found in virtually every aspect of societal living. We have heard about the cycles of the moon and sun and seasons, the fine line between idiot and genius at the top of the circle, the cycle of poverty, the inner circles of power, the aging cycle, and thousands of other cyclical patterns that make up this thing we call living. So the ripples form the small circle and then move out wider and move over us, drawing us into the circle.

A relatively new friend told me just a few weeks ago that he had never really made a full commitment to Christ even though he has attended church and been part of church life for several years. I was humbled beyond words when he told me that my service to God in going to Kenya had led him to make a true and lasting commitment to serve God himself in ways he never thought he would be doing. He shared with me how my example had led him into the deeper water with Christ and made his life so much richer and more meaningful because of his new relationship with God. He is one of my ripples. There will be others. I have no doubt about that. The Lord has set it up that way in using me as that *"pebble. "*

"Who will go for me? Whom shall I send?" The question is ever before us. Yes, there is so much to do. No, the problems can never be fully eliminated. There will always be people who are homeless, poor, hungry, diseased, uneducated, suffering, lost, denied, disenfranchised in every way imaginable. But Christ compels us to take action anyway, in whatever way we can, no matter how small. Christ did not eliminate hunger and poverty during his lifetime either. But His Great Commission to spread the Good News throughout the world includes an exemplary directive to serve others as He served. You don't have to go Kenya to do that *(unless, of course, God sends you an email).* It is simply a

matter of making a conscious choice, a living commitment, to share all good blessings with others whose hearts are weary with want and need.

I was 14 years old when I heard my first Simon and Garfunkel song. My transformation to today began at that moment in time, and over the years I have evolved with their music. I can remember a day in junior high school when I stood on a street corner three blocks from my house waiting for a friend to meet me. It was a cold, windy day in the fall. In the waiting, on my transistor radio, I heard *"The Sound of Silence"* for the very first time, and I somehow understood with clarity *"silence like a cancer grows...take my words that I might teach you, take my arms that I might reach you."* As much as the Bible molded me in those early childhood years of Sunday School and Vacation Bible School, my formative teenage years were chiseled by the music of that time. Those early Bible lessons and the poetic music continue to chip away at me today because they are still at the core of my belief system and values. *"The Sound of Silence"* still remains a song fresh to me even now when I hear it again. It never fails to make me stop and think about my purpose in life, my career with children and their teachers, and how much I have *"been made new"* over and over again.

I began this journal journey with the question in my mind about what purpose I might serve in going to

Kenya. Today it all seems so clear. I was to become the pebble to break the silence of the still, dirty, and unclean water that daily takes the lives of children and their parents. I was to become the pebble dropped into smooth, clear water of our blessed lives here. I was to work with the water in my own transformation – from rock – to pebble – and back again, now to become the cornerstone of a bridge. "

> *"When you're down and out,*
> *When you're on the street,*
> *When evening falls so hard, I will*
> *comfort you..."*
> – Bridge Over Troubled Water

`   Our God is a Mighty God! Just look at the circles that now overlap just because He dropped a little rock in the water of Kenya. Bwana asifiwe!

Chapter 12
Rock of Ages

Christians, by nature, through scripture, in studies and discussion, for their full understanding, have long associated Christ with water—the water of baptism, the Living Water, the Water that washes away all sin, and numerous other allusions and analogies and metaphors to strengthen the concept. When you stop to think about it though, rocks are as rich in religious symbolism as water is. On Christ the solid rock I stand. Remember Peter, the rock upon which Christ built the Church. The rock in David's slingshot killed Goliath, the giant, to represent the concept that *"in God all things are possible."* There is the country song with lyrics, *"Rockin' chairs, rockin' babies, rock-a-bye, and Rock of Ages."* So my last chapter was devoted to rocks and their place in the Big Scheme of Things. Or I should say, I thought that last chapter was my last chapter, but the story did not end there. I am not sure this whole story will ever completely come to an end. But I had a rock experience the other day that was so compelling, by necessity it had to be included in this book as another chapter although this one is being written about five months after that false conclusion.

It has now been a year and two months since I traveled to Africa and returned. Close to the anniversary date of that trip, word arrived that Bishop Mbai was coming to America on a mission to raise funds for a real dormitory for the Nairobi street boys who live at the Fountain of Life tent mission. I met Bishop Mbai and his assistant Gideon when I visited the tent mission with the 2003 LWI team. You may remember them from the earlier Chapter 4 about the robbers.

Since I last saw the Bishop, several significant things have happened to improve the life of the boys at the tent. The Bishop has rescued 3 more boys to live at the tent mission, and the government had promised him some beds for the boys if he could get a dormitory built. Several of the 2004 LWI team members, after visiting the tent mission in July, extended invitations to come and stay with them if he ever got back to America. He had come here once before, three years prior, when he came to raise money to buy the big circus tent that serves as his church. Take a moment and try to imagine yourself traveling thousands of miles, talking to hundreds of strangers, having no definitive place to stay, asking strangers for money, and trying to sell them on the idea of a circus tent church in a foreign country. As ridiculous as that scenario sounds, the Bishop was successful on that trip and that is how he got the tent mission started in the first place. Now he had another mission. He would come to America a second time, stay with some of the missioners who had issued invitations, and he would raise money for the new dormitory.

So in October he returned to America and came to visit many of us. He arrived with no definitive itinerary for housing and food. He came purely on faith that the Lord would open doors and hearts. He talked at many of our Sunday school classes and preached in our churches and told about the boys and the tent mission. He told us how the boys had come from the mean streets where they fought with goats and wild dogs and other animals and people for food to survive. He talked about their darkness and loneliness as each night each boy was forced to find his own shelter and comfort. He talked about the wildness of the boys, how uncivilized and animalistic they were when they first came to him. He talked about their training and rehabilitation. Homes and hearts opened up and money came in.

In the middle of his journey, however, Bishop Mbai became gravely ill with congestive heart failure and had to be hospitalized. God had all the bases covered though because a team member was able to find a physician, a cardiologist in fact, who was willing to test and treat the Bishop free of charge and also arranged for his hospitalization and medications as well. We were all very concerned, but the Bishop was not. He could see God's plan. Had the Lord not put it on his heart to come to America to raise money for the dormitory, he would have fallen ill in Nairobi. He told us he would surely have died had this happened in Kenya, and it was at this point I began to see how this plan for the Bishop was set in motion many months before this trip was even conceived. A rock was dropped into the water a long time back, and the ripples had just begun to move over all of us.

In October of 2003, when I left to go to Kenya and to meet the Bishop, I had no idea why God had pressed me so hard to go. When one of the preachers at the tent mission preached the message, *"Someone is waiting for you to set him free with the word of the Lord,"* I had no idea why such a simple message had such a strong impact on me. Now all the pieces of the puzzle were coming together, and it involved my good friend Brian, whom I barely knew before going to Kenya.

Brian attended church with me, but we were barely acquainted. After I told the stories of Kenya in a presentation at my church, Brian and I began talking more and more as his interest in going to Kenya on the next mission trip grew with dizzying intensity. About this same time, he told me he had begun his conversion to true faith. He said he had always attended church, but he had never really made a full commitment to Christ until sometime shortly after those presentations. I guess, just like God took hold on me and would not accept no as an answer, He found a way to get Brian's attention, too. I had been assigned the role of *"attention-getter"* or the *"tail twister"*, depending on the perspective. I recalled the words preached at the tent mission my last Sunday in Nairobi: *"Someone is waiting for you to set him free."* Brian was that someone waiting; and without my knowledge or intentional intervention, God set about the work of using my words and my experiences to draw Brian closer.

It wasn't long before Brian was signed on with the July 2004 mission, and he was *"chomping at the bit"* as we say in Texas, ready to leave, the time not passing fast enough for departure. July finally arrived and off he went to meet Miss Lucy and Bishop Mbai and many other Kenyans whose Christian example helped to mold further his faith and his desire to serve God. A surprise turn of events, though, awaited his return, and not long after his return from Kenya, Brian stopped coming to Holy Trinity. He became a member at another church that he felt better fit his needs for scripture and nourishment. It is far too personal to say how I felt about his leaving, about his leaving so soon after his mission, about his leaving because of some differing fundamental issues, about his leaving to grow elsewhere. Suffice it to say I felt deeply saddened, and it felt personal. I missed him. I missed his family. I missed his energy and his enthusiasm. While I was happy for him that he was finding what he was seeking in his spiritual life, nonetheless, I viewed it as both a personal loss and a spiritual loss. With Bishop Mbai's trip and illness, though, I quickly came to see the necessity of his having left and to see in real life an example of what it means that *"all things work for the good of the Lord."*

It was like some cosmic progression in an expanding universe, or something as simplistic as a chain of events strung together like popcorn on needle and thread.

  a. I meet Brian at church, and I meet Mbai in Kenya.
  b. Brian goes to Kenya after my trip and meets Mbai.
  c. Brian finds a new church and meets a cardiologist.
  d. Mbai comes to America, gets ill, and needs a cardiologist.
  e. Brian connects Mbai and the cardiologist.
  f. Mbai's health is restored, and the tent mission goes on.

There is that one simple algebra thing I understand: $A + B = C$. And this whole cycle started when I said yes to God when He called. Had I said no, I am sure God would have figured out another plan that would render the same final result, but it truly humbles me to think of the wonderful things that can be accomplished when we willingly (or even unwillingly) say yes to God. I had asked God if He was sure I was the one He wanted to go. He gave me the answer by letting me see that series of events play out in real time. Then for added measure, because He loves to play with me, He did one other little miracle. I was on my way to the hospital after work to see the Bishop. It had been a hard day at work, and driving was difficult, too, because of a 25 mph wind. I have my own health issues interfering with my energy and attitude. I was feeling irritable and harried and had several stops to make along the way because I wanted to take some things to the Bishop to make his hospital stay a little easier. I was racing along FM741, having passed numerous slow vehicles, cussing each one for getting in the way and slowing me down....

At last I saw open road, and I let the hammer down! As I approached a subdivision, though, a concrete pump truck with the big boom arm on it pulled out onto the highway doing 20 miles an hour in the 55 zone. I applied the brakes and was on his bumper as we approached a 3-way stop sign where you make the last turn to go into the town of Rockwall. Putt, putt, putt, putt...still twenty miles an hour along a section of road where there is a long no passing zone. I drove along at the snail's pass, tailgating, cussing, driving one handed. Who needs both hands on the wheel when you are only going 15-20 mph? Suddenly, a rock the size of quarter floated, literally floated in the wind, off the bumper of the concrete truck and gently landed on the hood of my car! Had we been driving the normal speed of 55 mph, it surely would have hit my windshield and cracked it all to pieces. But that rock set down on the hood of my car as gently as a grandmother lays a baby down for a nap, and it just sat there.

I laughed out loud, thinking, *"Ok, what an ingenious way to remind me to be a rock and not a butthole."* It was a reminder to be strong, a sign to slow down, a strong suggestion to be impervious to life's annoyances, and a directive to appreciate the opportunities to sit back, relax, and serve. I said a little prayer, *"Thanks for talking to me gently and not busting my windshield to pieces to get my attention."*

I expected the rock to roll off the hood as I drove along, but it stayed in position. I decided that when I got to a spot where I could pull off the road that I would do just that...and that I would collect the rock and keep it as a treasure of the moment. It rode on the hood for a long way, all the way into town, past the trees and gardens, past fences, churches, and high dollar housing. I drove stealthily to help keep it in place, and as I turned off the road...gently, slowly, deftly, so as not to sling off the magic rock, I diverted my eyes for one split second. I turned the wheels and pulled to a stop. The rock was gone. I had not seen it slide off. I had not heard it rattle and slide off. I got out and looked around but did not see any rock resembling it. It seemingly had just disappeared...a true magic rock. What a treasure it would have been to keep...better even than a midnight blue agate shooter, better even than a box of tiny bream hooks. The rock was gone, but the lesson was not lost.

As of this moment, the Bishop is back in Nairobi with his family. His mission was successful enough to garner funds plentiful enough to double his facilities. He should soon be able to take in another 35-50 boys, and he will be receiving regular assistance through several churches here that he visited. Bishop Mbai walked each day, through sickness and health, with no agenda other than to do God's work and go where God led. It is amazing to see the hand of the Lord at work in such profound abundance. Again, Bwana asifiwe!

There is no doubt in my mind that God speaks to Pastor Mbai. There is no doubt in my mind that He speaks to each of us at one time or another. I have had the good fortune to share several good conversations with Him lately. Again, there was no burning bush, no bright blinding light, no smoke on the mountain...just a rock that didn't hit the windshield.

Chapter 13
Bible Realities

I keep going back to the stories I have written here, and each time I do, there is something new to be extracted. It was 2003 when I set foot on Kenyan soil, and it was 2012 when I wrote this last chapter. But time has not withered those experiences; Kenya and the people are still a part of my daily thoughts and prayers. If anything, time has polished those memories and brought deeper revelation to the things I saw and learned there.

Much has taken place during these passing years, as one might expect. Following Bishop Mbai's successful 2004 trip to the U.S. to raise money for the dormitory at the Tent Mission, a group of missioners went over in 2005 and helped make several improvements to the property. The dorm was well in progress. A kitchen and dining hall had been built. A $30,000 borehole infrastructure was being constructed so the boys would have access to clean water. The future was looking very bright for the boys at the Tent Mission. Then the year of hard times began.

Spring came in 2006, and on May 25, the Lord's mighty servant, Bishop Mbai, was called home to meet his Maker. The Bishop's untimely death was both shocking and crushing, and it left the future of the ministry in question, but only briefly. Bishop Mbai's wife, Florence, and his son, Lameck, took up the mantle and decided they would continue the Bishop's great work of feeding, sheltering, and educating the orphans taken from the streets.

But then a darkness fell that shook everyone to the core. At 10 pm on December 19, 2006, just before Christmas, a group of approximately 50 angry, young Muslim men entered the compound with bulldozers and destroyed everything within the walls of the Tent Mission. All the buildings were literally bulldozed to the ground! Despite the fact that the government had given letters of allotment to the church, it seems the Muslims had convinced or bribed the authorities to allow them permission to take over this ground. The entire compound was destroyed under the watchful eyes of the Kenyan police. Gideon, the boys, the teachers, all were powerless to stop the raid.

Nothing was left but rubble when the marauders finally left the mission. The classrooms were gone. The dorm was gone. The tent was gone. The cook house was gone. The garden was gone. The fence, the gate, all of their security was gone. The expensive borehole that offered so much hope was gone. The peace was broken. It was a more desperate time than usual for the mission and those who depended on its survival.

But Christmas came and went, and the boys, though heavily traumatized by the destruction of the only place they knew as home, were taken in by others and sheltered and fed. The blessing of not having to return to the streets was the best Christmas gift of all.

So yet again we see modern proof that God is ever faithful as He provided the encouragement and strength needed to rebuild and start anew. The incomprehensible demolition of the orphanage made the news two years ago, and new strangers, some from the International Justice Mission, stepped forward to help in the crisis by finding lawyers to take the mission's case to court to gain restitution. Today those at the mission are no worse off than when I met with them in 2003, but much progress was lost. Rebuilding will be slow, but forgiveness came swiftly. Those leading the mission continue today to live among the Muslims, to minister to them, to love them....dangerous as it is to do so. The compassion far outweighs the fear. The mission's work continues and the goal remains intact: orphans rescued, local church strengthened, God's kingdom expanded. The vision is no dimmer.

So what have we here with these stories? For most we have a modern day version that correlates to some ancient Bible story we learned in Sunday School during our childhood. For the city of Nairobi, there is the Tower of Babel story. For Living Water there is the entire life of Christ and his work and teaching among the sick and poor. For the Maasai there is the story of David and his courage to face the giant Goliath, just as the Maasai daily face the lions and encroaching civilization. Pehucci and the Tent Mission are clearly both about Good Samaritans saving the lives of strangers on the street. The story of Brian shows the faith of the mustard seed. He has indeed been able to move mountains to enrich the lives of the boys at the Tent Mission, to which he has dedicated his time and energy. The safari I can equate with nothing less than the story of Daniel in the lions' den.

These stories give but a small, small glimpse though of the enormous experience I had doing mission work in Kenya. Hopefully the stories have made a difference of some kind in your faith so that you will move into action the way Brian did. No matter how little you do for the hungry, the needy, the sick, the homeless, the struggling survivors...each portion helps them through one more day. Do what you can; don't be afraid to get involved. When you step out of your fear, incredible things can happen in your life.

And so I close with one more quick story. It is about one of the tent mission boys I will long remember even though I don't know his real name. I call him Elijah. He was very small, maybe five years old. That last Sunday we were in Nairobi we went to the tent mission for church services. It was very hot that morning, very hot, and even though the sides of the tent were tied up, there was no breeze to be had. You may recall in an earlier story I mentioned there were four preachers that morning, so the service was quite long.

I was sweating quite a lot, and because of the discomfort I was unaccustomed to, I was having trouble concentrating by the middle of the third sermon. Suddenly a little boy from the mission came up and sat beside me. Without saying a word, he snuggled in as close to me as he could get without actually sitting in my lap. He looked up at me and smiled. I put my arm around his shoulder, and he scooted in even closer. It got even hotter, being so close to each other, and both of us sweated even more. Despite the discomfort though, we stayed like that for a long time. By the time the fourth sermon began, he was asleep, propped against me, sound asleep. I like to think a sense of safety made it possible for him to sleep there beside me under my wing. I had a chance to be the good kind of sheltering *"rock"* again. So the discomfort was worth every sweat bead.

I can't even imagine the courage it took for this small boy to approach me, a total stranger, and to seek from me some comfort that could bring such a deep and blissful sleep as that which he had that morning. Whatever fear he had, though, he simply ignored it and took the chance. Few of us step out of our fear to take those big chances in life. I just know I am far richer for having overcome my fear and stepping out. My experiences in Kenya remind me of that Tim McGraw song about getting the chance to *live like you were dying* but then living to tell about it. I had that experience in Kenya, and these stories are my testament to the wonder and awe of God at work in our lives even today...even still. Many may doubt that He is involved with us in this modern, technological world because we don't see burning bushes and pillars of fire any more. But I am convinced He is closer than ever. I have the email to prove it.

G.E. Johnson

Born and raised in Jackson and coming of age during the early years of the Civil Rights Movement, Johnson was a first hand eyewitness to the violence and upheaval that turned a national spotlight on Mississippi. Finding a talent for writing as a teen, Johnson always knew a book was in the future, but a 40 year career in public education as both teacher and administrator took priority. That career began in the infamous town of Money, MS where the Emmett Till murder story began. Those early years impacted Johnson in a profound way as even today this writer remains in the ranks of those still pushing back against racism and inequality.

Johnson graduated from Jackson Central High School and received both a Bachelors and Masters degree from Delta State University in Cleveland, MS. The writer has lived in Texas for the past 35 years but has never forgotten the roots set down while growing up in the Magnolia State.

Her first novel *Darkness on the Delta* is also available on Amazon. Johnson is also hard at work on her next book.